DRAWING
A STUDY GUIDE

a supplement to DRAWING

Daniel M. Mendelowitz

Stanford University

HOLT, RINEHART AND WINSTON, INC.

NEW YORK · CHICAGO · SAN FRANCISCO · TORONTO · LONDON

FOREWORD

D RAWING: A *Study Guide* presents a variety of problems, procedures, and experiences planned to assist the beginner in learning to draw and to become familiar with the scope of drawing. It is designed to be used in close conjunction with the author's larger volume, *Drawing*. More specifically, this study guide has been planned to translate the general and theoretical concepts presented in *Drawing* into specific activities suitable either for classroom or independent use.

Many teachers rely on a core of favorite problems and procedures. The projects presented here have been conceived to reinforce or replace familiar and traditional classroom activities. They are based on Chapters 1 and 13 through 18 of *Drawing*. Reading of Chapters 2 through 12 on the history of drawing is not assigned; these chapters nevertheless should be read as soon as possible since they provide general background for the drawing exercises. One of the special aims of this pair of books is to integrate studio instruction in drawing and art history in a meaningful way. The author's intent is not to outline a course in drawing but to design a range of basic experiences on which teachers may depend to supplement their own special strengths and extend students' talents and interests.

Students working without a teacher will probably find it advisable to carry out the suggested projects in the order in which they appear. Even if all of these are not executed, the assignments should be read carefully so that the concept presented in the project is understood. As the independent student develops skills, confidence, and intensive interests, he may wish to concentrate on one type of drawing, one medium, or one type of subject. It is likely, then, that many of the suggested activities may seem to divert him from his evolving areas of specialization and will therefore appear distracting and irrelevant. When this occurs the student will be wise to concentrate on the area of his special interest and develop it intensively. It is the author's contention that growth in depth is more important to artistic development than growth in breadth. Breadth of experience serves the primary function of helping the individual find himself.

It is true, however, that any serious and intensive activity eventually demands an expansion of horizons. The beginner has constantly to guard against the tendency to buttress his emerging artistic ego by repeating minor successes and thus neglect the discovery of his full strengths and capacities. The work of most mature artists reveals periods of intensive concentration within a narrow framework of special concerns and problems alternating with periods of exploration and experimentation. The beginner will be wise to travel a similar path; concentrate on areas of special interest as long as they remain challenging but, when success comes too easily, move on. Exploration in breadth combined with concentration in depth requires the particular discipline which characterizes the artist: an inner discipline in which deep satisfactions and dynamic dissatisfactions alternate to stimulate continual growth. Through such a discipline the art student discovers and reveals himself and thereby establishes the basis for becoming an artist.

Daniel M. Mendelowitz

Stanford University
Stanford, California
July 1, 1966

CONTENTS

part 1

INITIAL EXPERIENCES

Beginners should not attempt to use media that demand great skill. It is important to draw as uninhibitedly as possible so that the transmission of impressions, ideas, and impulses is direct and unself-conscious. Pencil, charcoal, and brush and ink are excellent media with which to begin to draw and should meet initial needs. Beginners will require the following equipment and materials to commence working; other media, materials, and tools can be added later.

■ *Materials for Beginners*

> DRAWING BOARD (*basswood*), *20 inches by 26 inches*
>
> THUMB TACKS (*to hold individual pieces of paper to the drawing board*)
>
> HEAVY CLIPS (*to hold the newsprint pad to the drawing board*)
>
> NEWSPRINT PAD (*18 by 24*)
>
> 4B OR 6B GRAPHITE DRAWING PENCIL
>
> LARGE SOFT ERASER (*for pencil*)
>
> STICK CHARCOAL (*soft*) *and compressed charcoal* (*0 or 00*)
>
> KNEADED ERASER
>
> CHAMOIS
>
> FIXATIF (*Fixatif blower if fixatif does not come in pressurized cans*)
>
> INDIA INK
>
> MEDIUM-SIZED POINTED BRUSH (*No. 10*), *of the best quality you can afford.*

1

1a. *Charcoal*
applied with the side of the stick.

■ Media for Beginners

1b. *Diagonal charcoal lines*
applied with the point of the stick.

1c. *Charcoal lines*
cross-hatched
with the point of the stick.

Before commencing this project read in *Drawing*, Chapter 16, *The Dry Media*. In Chapter 17, *The Wet Media*, read the section on Brush and Ink, page 405.

All details discussed and shown in this book are from complete works reproduced in color or black and white in the author's volume *Drawing*. Pertinent information about media, dimensions, and the artists will be found there.

Project One

BEGINNERS' MEDIA: CHARCOAL

Charcoal is easy to apply, easy to remove, can be used for line drawing (by pointing the stick) or for value studies (by using the side of the piece or by applying sets of parallel or cross-hatched lines). (Figure 1.) When grays with a minimum of texture are desired, parallel lines or cross-hatched textures can be fused by rubbing gently with the fingers, with soft paper, or by using a tortillon or paper stump. To practice using charcoal, draw lines, rapidly sketched clusters of diagonal parallel lines, and cross-hatched tones with a pointed piece of charcoal. Using the side of a piece of charcoal, build a smoothly graduated value from black to very light gray. Do the same with lines fused with your finger, reinforced by subsequent applications of charcoal and rubbing. Study the details of the following drawings for the use of charcoal: Millet's "Man with a Barrow" (Figure 2), Degas' "Groupe de Danseuses Vues en Buste" (Figure 3), Seurat's "Sous le Lampe" (Figure 74c), Prud'hon's "Head of a Woman (Marguerite)" (Figure 4). See if you can duplicate the effects found

1d. *Charcoal lines*
fused by rubbing.

2. *Charcoal. Firm, simple contours.*
Values built by basically parallel lines.
Detail of "Man with Barrow," Jean François Millet.
For complete drawing and caption see Drawing, *Figure 16–1.*
Alinari-Art Reference Bureau.

3. Charcoal. Free outlines.
Values built through parallel and cross-hatched lines.
Detail of "Groupe de Danseuses Vues en Buste," Edgar Degas.
See Drawing, Figure 16–2. Allen Memorial Art Museum,
Oberlin College, Ohio (Friends of Art Fund).

INITIAL EXPERIENCES

*4. Charcoal. Smooth value gradations
created by disciplined applications of charcoal and rubbing.
Detail of "Head of a Woman (Marguerite)," Pierre-Paul Prud'hon.
See Drawing, Figure 16–5.
Art Institute of Chicago (The Simeon D. Williams Fund).*

5. Pencil outline.
Modulated widths. Detail of
"The Bathers," Pablo Picasso.
See Drawing, *Figure 10–5.*
Fogg Art Museum, Cambridge,
Mass. (Meta and Paul J.
Sachs Collection).

in these drawings. You might profitably copy a part of each. For the full drawings, information on the medium and sizes of the originals as well as dates and nationalities of the artists, see *Drawing*.

Many *chalks* are very similar to charcoal (compressed charcoal is often classified as chalk) except that they tend to be harder to erase. Each of the above projects can also be executed in chalk.

Project Two

BEGINNERS' MEDIA: PENCIL

The virtue of pencil is that it is familiar and relatively clean. Sharpen your pencil and scribble freely on a sheet of newsprint paper. Observe the quality of line produced by using the point of the pencil, by using the side of the lead. Observe the difference in line quality achieved by using the pencil in an upright position (as in writing) and holding it between the thumb and forefinger but *under* your hand. The latter position is preferred by most artists because it is easier to vary the thickness of the line since a slight shift of hand position utilizes either the point or the side of the lead. Study the details from Picasso's "The Bathers" (Figure 5), Degas' "Gentleman Rider" (Figure 6), Constable's "Poplars by a Stream" (Figure 7), Gleizes' "Port" (Figure 39) and Maillol's "Two Figures" (Figure 8). See if you can duplicate the kinds of lines, textures, and values you see in those drawings. You would probably profit from copying a part of each. Study the full drawings in *Drawing*.

INITIAL EXPERIENCES

6. Pencil line.
Clustered lines to suggest form.
Detail from "Gentleman Rider,"
Edgar Degas. See Drawing,
Figure 16–9 Art Institute of
Chicago (The Charles Deering
Collection).

Project Three

BEGINNERS' MEDIA: BRUSH AND INK

Brush and ink demand a certain assurance since lines cannot be
erased. The bold lines that result when brush and India ink are used
freely give a certain authority to a drawing, and the self-confidence
that results from the successful use of the brush is most valuable. To
draw with brush and ink, dip your brush in India ink and then gently
press the brush against the side of the bottle neck to remove excess
ink and point the brush. Practice making graduated lines with brush
and ink. Observe the use of this medium in Rivera's "Mother and
Child" (Figure 9) and in Hokusai's "The Mochi Makers" (Figure
30). Copy a part of each drawing. Do not strive for an exact copy,
but try to duplicate the quality of the brushed-ink lines. The full
drawings are reproduced in *Drawing*, Figures 9–9, 17–8. In the
following assignments, unless the medium is specified, use the medium of your choice.

Initial Experiences: Learning to See

Read Chapter 1 of *Drawing*. Three types of drawing are identified: (1) drawings that record what is seen; (2) drawings that visualize what is imagined; and (3) drawings that symbolize ideas and concepts. These aspects of drawing do not exclude one another; in fact, the greatest drawings, such as Michelangelo's "Archers Shooting at Mark" (*Drawing*, Figure 3–14), achieve their full emotional power because of the grandeur with which they fulfill all three of these esthetic purposes.

Perhaps the most fundamental discipline involved in drawing is learning to record what is seen. Contrary to popular misconceptions, this is not primarily a matter of manual skills. The physical requisites for drawing are minimal: average sight and average manual dexterity. Drawing is a matter of seeing through the mind, of comprehension, rather than of 20–20 vision and deft fingers. Here we are not considering the requisites for being an original or powerful artist but rather the skill and habits involved in being an adequate draftsman, the kind of person who can look at an object, analyze quickly the relationship of size, shape, value, and texture he sees, and create an analogous set of relationships on paper which graphically describe his perceptions.

Let us analyze what differentiates the seeing involved in learning to draw from the seeing that enables us to move about and identify objects in daily life. We exist from birth in spatial depth; that is, we live in a three-dimensional world in which we move freely back, forth, up, down, in space, and around objects. From childhood on our hands, bodies, and most of all, our eyes—placed-in-our-swivel-pivoting-head—appraise objects in terms of their three-dimensional character. This is how we know them. It is, therefore, frequently difficult for a beginner drawing a cube placed at eye level not to attempt to show the top plane of the cube, because he knows that it is there even though he cannot see it. When we commence to draw, it comes as a shock to discover that any object except a sphere pre-

7. Pencil dark and light.
Detail from "Poplars by a Stream," John Constable.
See Drawing, Figure 7–14.
Henry E. Huntington Library and Art Gallery, San Marino.

8. *Pencil. Value relationships and form*
built by scribbled encompassing line.
Detail from "Two Figures," Aristide Maillol.
See Drawing, *Figure 13–17.*
Achenbach Foundation for Graphic Arts,
California Palace of the Legion of Honor, San Francisco.

9. Brush and ink.
Heavy, freely modulated lines.
Detail from "Mother and Child,"
Diego Rivera. See Drawing,
Figure 17–8. San Francisco
Museum of Art (Albert M. Bender Collection).

sents a different appearance whenever we change the position of our eyes in relation to it: the beginning draftsman is faced with a new problem. Three-dimensional knowledge must be re-evaluated; translated into two-dimensional patterns based on a fixed relationship between the draftsman's eyes and the object. Actual spatial depth being absent from the surface of the drawing paper, three-dimensional reality must be translated into a two-dimensional pattern. Thus much of learning to draw consists of discovering how things *appear* rather than of how they are, and it is not until we begin to draw that most of us discover the tremendous difference between what we know about objects and what we see.

Learning to draw, then, demands a re-evaluation of visual experience, becoming primarily dependent upon visual cues as to the appearances of objects and their relationships in space. You already have certain resources which you can use when confronted with a drawing problem. If you are asked to draw three circles in space so they appear in front of one another, you might produce something like Figure 10. If you are asked to repeat the project but make the circles appear to be a great distance from one another, you might come up with something like Figure 11. In both instances you would draw upon your knowledge of seeing and employ devices that derive solely from seeing. The two familiar concepts embodied in Figures 10 and

10. *Overlapping forms
create a sense of space.*

11 are: (1) when we see a sequence of objects in space the objects in front can partially obscure (overlap) the objects in back; (2) the more distant objects are from the viewer, the smaller they appear. (Think how you shift your head in a motion picture theatre to keep the relatively small head immediately in front of you from obscuring most of the giant screen.) Both of these aspects of drawing-related-to-seeing are common knowledge and can be observed without any special training, but when we try to describe more subtle phenomena the problems become more difficult. The following projects are designed to introduce certain habits of observation and certain simple perspective and foreshortening concepts.

Project Four

LEARNING TO SEE: OVERLAPPING FORMS, DIMINISHING SIZES, "LAYERED SPACE"

Using soft pencil, enclose four rectangular areas about the size of the *Study Guide* (you might just draw around it) on a piece of newsprint. In rectangle No. 1: draw a series of overlapping circular forms that do not have important differences in size. In rectangle No. 2: draw forms that overlap and diminish in size as they seem to recede to intensify the sense of intervening distance. In rectangle No. 3: draw a series of forms of approximately the same size using "layered" or "tiered" space (*Drawing*, page 322). That is, place the front overlapping forms at the bottom; have the successive overlapped forms placed higher in the composition as they recede. In rectangle No. 4: draw a sequence of forms using overlapping, diminishing sizes and placement in the composition ("layered space") to give the maximum sense of space.

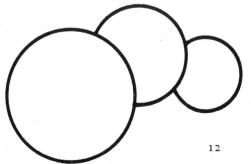

11. *Diminishing sizes
reinforce overlapping forms
to intensify the
sense of intervening distance.*

INITIAL EXPERIENCES

12. Foreshortening.
*Detail from "Study for the Dead Body
of Acron," Jean-Auguste Dominique Ingres.
See* Drawing, Figure 1–10.
Metropolitan Museum of Art,
New York (Rogers Fund, 1919).

Project Five

LEARNING TO SEE: FORESHORTENING

Overlapping, diminishing sizes, and "layered space" devices used in the previous project are means for describing objects in space rather than picturing the changes that occur when we see an individual object from different viewpoints. Below is a project designed to stimulate the beginner to observe the changes in the appearance of a single object that occur when the viewpoint is altered. A body of principles exists to describe such changes, as well as to depict objects in deep space in a systematic way. This body of principles is termed *perspective*. Frequently the word *perspective* is used when referring to geometric and architectural forms, while *foreshortening* is preferred to describe the perspective of organic or anatomical forms. Good illustrations of foreshortened forms can be observed in "Study for the Deady Body of Acron" by Ingres (Figure 12) and "Studies of a Cat" by Géricault (Figure 13).

13. *Foreshortening.*
Detail of "Studies of a Cat,"
Théodore Géricault. See Drawing,
Figure 16–10. Fogg Art Museum,
Cambridge, Mass.

Select a large, not-too-flat leaf that is fairly rigid, preferably with undulating edges (a magnolia or calla lily leaf is excellent). Study it full face and analyze its general shape and its proportions of length to width. (1) Draw it full face, about life size, in the medium of your choice. (2) Turn the leaf back-side to you and repeat the performance. Some of the edges will appear very different while the general proportions may or may not be the same. Try to be equally aware of the general shape and the undulations of edge. (3) Turn the leaf in a flat, sideways position so that you see its full length but its width disappears through foreshortening. In this position you may be sharply aware of the undulating edge since you may see parts of the top and the bottom of the leaf at the same time. Now turn the leaf so that its end comes directly toward you. Notice how its length disappears and you become aware of the twistings and turnings of the edges (Figure 14). Sketch the leaf in any other positions that intrigue you, noticing the constantly varying relationships of shape, size, and proportion of parts. Take a branch with three or four leaves on it and draw the cluster. Make a similar sequence of drawings of some fairly large, solid organic object: a bone, a squash, a large, firm cabbage with one leaf turned out from the head. Most important in this and subsequent projects is to repeatedly look at what you are drawing. It is easy to become absorbed in the act of drawing and, ceasing to observe, gradually draw from *idea* rather than from visual analysis.

INITIAL EXPERIENCES

14. *Foreshortening.*
Calla Lily Leaf.
Side view and end view.

Project Six

LEARNING TO SEE: FORESHORTENED GEOMETRIC FORMS

Beginners frequently find it easier to draw simple organic shapes in foreshortening than more precise geometric forms. Perhaps this is because the draftsman has a more clear and exact idea of the actual form of the geometric object in his mind and therefore does not *have* to look so continuously at the object to determine its appearance. Drawing the *Study Guide* provides an introductory exercise in the foreshortening of simple rectangular forms. Place the book directly in front of you slightly below eye level. Study its appearance carefully, then try to draw it in simple outline. The result should look similar to Figure 15a. However, some individuals may find it difficult to represent the lengthened rectangle of the page by means

15. *Foreshortening.*
(a) Study Guide *seen in foreshortening close to eye level.*
(b) *Actual proportions of book.*
(c) *Book drawn in isometric perspective.*

of a nonrectangular horizontal shape. That is because you know the proportions of the form to be like Figure 15b, so you find it difficult to see the proportions and shapes in Figure 15c. Your factual knowledge of the actual proportions blocks your visual perception and makes it difficult to estimate the shapes you see.

Place the book to one side of you, slightly below eye level. Again trying to estimate the exact shapes you see, make a simple outline drawing. If you draw the receding edges of the pages parallel to one another, as beginners frequently do, you will approximate isometric perspective in your treatment of space (*Drawing*, page 333). Such a drawing might resemble Figure 15c. If your lines representing the receding edges of the pages tend to converge, you will be suggesting space by means of conventional Western perspective. Draw the book in a number of positions at varying levels using both isometric and converging perspective.

We have been working with relatively simple forms to acquaint the beginning student of drawing with habits and concepts involved in representational drawing. The next drawing project involves more complex forms and introduces certain mechanical aids and procedures useful in determining relationships of size and shape. Though what we need to develop is eye, mind, and hand coordination, one should be familiar with any simple mechanical aids that can help ascertain the exact shapes and relationships we see. Sometimes such devices help to guide initial judgments when we are commencing a drawing, sometimes they help us find mistakes.

■ Learning to See: Mechanical Aids to Perception

Place a wooden chair in front of you in a number of positions—facing you, with its back to you, sideways, upside-down and at a tilted angle. Study it carefully in each position, preparing as though to draw it. Note the way the size and shape relationships between the

parts alter with each change of position. Before you complete the project you will draw this chair in a number of positions. But before you commence to draw, let us examine the previously mentioned mechanical aids that may contribute help.

■ *The Pencil Used as a Plumb Line*

A pencil held in a vertical position is very useful in ascertaining certain relationships and alignments (Figure 16a,b). Notice in Figure 16a the way in which the position of the pencil clearly reveals that the chair's front leg rests on the floor far left of the seat. If the pencil is moved so that it forms a plumb line on the left-hand side of the chair, it will reveal that the back rest is far to the right of the farther rear leg. Held in a true horizontal position, the pencil is equally useful in determining relationships of above and below. For instance, in Figure 16b, see how the forward position of the right forward leg is revealed by the horizontal plumb line as well as the placement in the drawing of the other three legs.

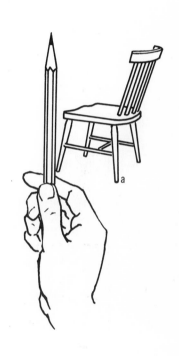

■ *The Pencil as a Measuring Device*

The pencil can not only be used as a plumb line to determine vertical and horizontal alignments, but it can also provide a device for determining relationships of shape and proportion. For instance, one might have difficulty in determining the proportion of height to width in the foreshortened seat of the chair. Holding the pencil at *full* arm's length, and allowing the tip of the pencil to touch the left-hand edge of the seat, mark with your thumbnail the right edge of the seat. (Be certain that the pencil is always held at *full* arm's length since any change in the distance between the pencil and the eye destroys the accuracy of the measurement.) Turn your pencil vertically, being certain to keep your thumbnail in place on the pen-

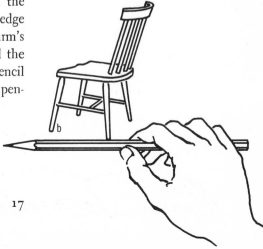

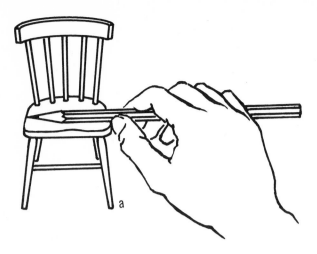

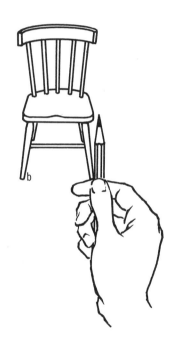

17a-b. *Pencil used to estimate size relationships.*

cil. Estimate the proportion of the marked width to the height. You can space it off if you find it difficult to estimate (Figure 17a,b).

■ A *Square Viewer*

Cut a one-inch square from a piece of light cardboard or stiff paper. Look at the chair you intend to draw through this hole, holding the paper as far from your eye as possible, still permitting the entire chair to be seen through the square aperture but filling the square as completely as possible. Notice how the square viewer enables you to see vertical, horizontal, and proportionate relationships. The negative spaces, the areas left between the edges of the square and the contours of the chair are also most helpful in determining what shapes you see (Figure 18). Observe the chair in a number of positions through the viewer and then proceed with the drawing assignment outlined below. Be certain to hold the viewer in a true vertical position.

Project Seven

LEARNING TO SEE: DRAWING A CHAIR IN FOUR DIFFERENT POSITIONS

A simple wooden chair provides an excellent exercise in drawing since it is made up of a number of parts of extremely varied shapes, its forms are not strictly geometric nor are they as subtle as anatomical or organic forms, and the legs, stretchers, and spindles provide excellent baffles through which other parts can be seen. Place the chair in the first position of your choice. Study the position carefully, consciously noticing any foreshortening of seat, back, legs, rungs, and so on. When you feel you understand the relationships, proceed to draw the chair rather rapidly, not worrying about accuracy in the depiction of thicknesses, taperings, straight edges, and so on, but simply attempting to describe the shapes and sizes of the main parts. Study the negative areas (the shapes you see between the rungs, between the legs, stretcher-bars, and other parts). These often provide new insights as to the accuracy of your drawing. For the successive drawings place the chair in as differing positions as possible. In each drawing it is necessary to observe your subject continuously as you draw. Most mistakes occur from drawing without looking at your model. The use of your pencil as a plumb line and of the cut-out square as a viewer should only be employed as a preliminary step to drawing, or to clarify a relationship of parts as you are working. Overdependence upon such aids can impede the development of independent judgments and of eye–hand coordination.

■ Learning to See: Sketchbook Activities

Form the habit of observing and sketching something every day. The habit and regular practice of sketching is essential to continuous development. In time the response of the hand to the eye is spontaneous. Carry a small sketchbook and set aside ten minutes each day to drawing whatever you see around you: people, automobiles, buildings, trees, shrubs, typewriters, your own hand or foot. Frequently objects that do not seem promising prove to be very interesting to draw. Your sketchbook can provide a vocabulary of forms, a continuous source of motifs and ideas for compositions, as well as an entertaining record of your past (a visual diary).

■ Initial Experiences: Learning to Visualize

Drawing provides an instrument not only for recording what is seen but also for visualizing what is in the mind. Such visualizations can be realistic, symbolic or diagrammatic. Just as the ability to draw that which is seen can be developed through practice so can the ability to visualize imagined forms. Many individuals become self-conscious and "block" when asked to draw from imagination. These same persons probably "doodle" freely, for when doodling they follow their own unconscious impulses with no concern about the artistic quality of their scribblings though doodlings frequently produce forms of considerable artistic interest.

18. A cut-out square used to estimate size relationships.

19. *Essentially scribbled forms enriched with details to create figures. Detail of "Figures," Joan Miró. See* Drawing, *Figure 18–12.* Feigen/Palmer Gallery, Inc., Los Angeles.

Project Eight

LEARNING TO VISUALIZE: DOODLING

The first step in learning to visualize is being able to draw upon your inner resources for forms and ideas without being dependent upon seeing an external model. Doodle for fifteen or twenty minutes. If you are self-conscious and cannot produce, look through notebooks, the fly-leaf and margins of old textbooks or any other likely sources and select from any doodles you find there motifs for the following: Enclose a few rectangles approximately 5 inches by 7 inches and, using pencil, compose in the first rectangle enlarged duplicates of some of your most interesting doodles. (In composing forms in a rectangle, having major forms touch the four edges of the rectangle intensifies the sense of composition for it relates these forms in a very positive way to the area in which they are placed.) You may be satisfied with your composed doodle. If not, freely add any elements that will suggest identifiable objects, give solidity or weight, or provide interesting contrasts or countermovements. Notice in Miró's "Figures" (Figure 19) how little it takes to make figures from scribbles! Repeat this performance in rectangle No. 2, changing your doodle motifs and their placement in the composition. In composition No. 2 consciously add to the original form to increase the sense of depth, solidity, or the suggestions of identifiable objects. Study Kandinsky's untitled drawing (Figure 20). It is in essence an elaborated doodle.

INITIAL EXPERIENCES

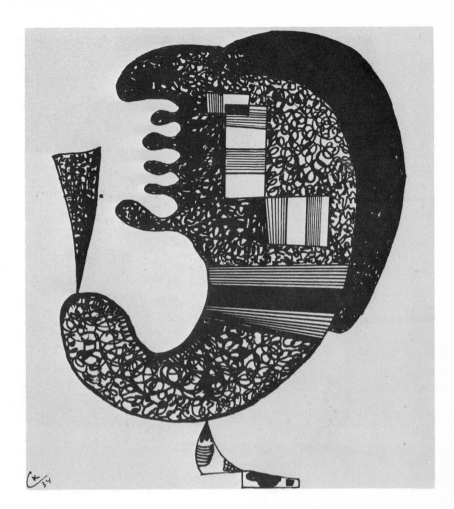

20. *A free shape enriched with doodled textures.* Untitled, *Wassily Kandinsky. See* Drawing, *Figure 18–18.* Feigen/Palmer Gallery, Inc., Los Angeles.

Project Nine

LEARNING TO VISUALIZE: DIAGRAMMATIC DRAWINGS

Most individuals can make a diagrammatic representation of an object if it is sufficiently familiar to them. They also usually have a vocabulary of forms which they can draw but hesitate to commit to paper as part of a serious class assignment because they do not feel their vocabulary of forms to be professional in quality. The following exercises are planned to encourage beginners to draw from imagination, as small children do, freely and without critical restraint. Try to work rapidly, and if you block on a problem, move on to the next and try returning to it later.

1. Enclose a series of approximately 5-inch by 7-inch rectangles and place the following problems in them. Draw a jagged shape with straight lines to express an explosion. Add lines, dots, small broken shapes and any other elements to intensify the sense of explosive energy. Continue the lines and movements to the edge of the rectangles to create a composition expressing explosion.

2. Draw two biomorphic shapes colliding. Add lines to suggest the movement that brought the two forms into conflict. Give evidence

of the impact by indentation, flying fragments, radial lines and any other devices you can create.

3. Compose a series of leaf shapes such as you drew in Project Five in as many different positions as you can conceive. Do not look at the leaves or your earlier drawing, but draw on memory (memory is the storehouse of imagination). Draw the leaves large and compose them so they touch the edges of the rectangle. By overlapping, foreshortening, and diminishing sizes, create a vigorous sense of space.

4. Draw two chairs floating in space. Overlap parts of the chairs so that a strong sense of depth is established. Try to arrange the chairs so that they appear to have been carried into the air by a cyclone.

5. Draw a flat, irregular geometric shape using straight lines to establish its boundaries. Make it three-dimensional by adding thickness. Draw circular holes into it (like holes in Swiss cheese). Draw spaghettilike rods looping through the holes and add any forms you wish that will give a sense of space and volume.

6. From imagination compose diagrammatic drawings of forms in three dimensions which reveal a cross-section. Use familiar objects, a cross-section of an orange showing segments and seeds, an apple cut in half lengthwise showing core and seeds, a section of automobile tire showing tread and varying thicknesses of casing, and so on. Add other cross-sections of the same or related object to create a composition.

■ Learning to Visualize: Sketchbook Activities

At the conclusion of projects on learning to see, it is suggested that you keep a sketchbook. Such a sketchbook should not be reserved exclusively for recording what you see but should encompass the full gamut of drawing activities. Alternate your drawing from models with drawing objects from memory. Certain habits can build skill at memory drawing. Look hard at an object, trying to fix its pro-

21. *Symbol drawing.*
Detail of "Improper Use of Government Property Is Frowned Upon," Maggie Wesley.
See Drawing,
Figure 1–16. Collection of the artist.

portions and relationships of parts in your mind and then draw without looking back. A second good visualizing exercise is to study an object and then draw it from another point of view, as though you were high above it, far below, or viewing it from the other side. Also doodle freely in your sketchbook, and then elaborate your favorites to make them more interesting. Kandinsky's untitled drawing (Figure 20) is an imagined form enriched with doodled textures.

■ Beginning Experiences: Learning to Symbolize

To symbolize means to represent by a symbol. Both things and qualities can be represented by symbols which may or may not have a physical resemblance to the object symbolized: the symbol for the crescent moon bears some resemblance to the crescent moon in shape, the symbol for a star represents a simplification of the effect of radiating light that emanates from a star; on the other hand the symbol for an electric outlet used in architectural plans bears no physical resemblance to an electric outlet. Symbols for nonphysical qualities cannot, of course, resemble the qualities they symbolize. The cross which symbolizes Christianity and the flag which symbolizes the United States illustrate this. The basic necessity for a successful symbol is that it be widely understood. Symbols are fre-

22. *Symbolic caricature.*
Detail of "A Group of Vultures Waiting for the Storm to 'Blow Over,' 'Let Us Prey,'"
Thomas Nast.
See Drawing, *Figure 12–3.* The New York Public Library.

quent in folk arts because they convey widely held and readily accepted meanings. Comic books and trade marks today, and the decorative patterns of folk arts and crafts in earlier times provided readily understood symbols for the people of the cultures that produced them. The symbols that are part of our national life become symbols because they provide an effective means of embodying a complex of ideas into a readily recognized form. Thus they provide a convenient shorthand for nonverbal visual communication. See how Maggie Wesley's weighty yet wittily formalized shapes produce an authoritative but light-hearted warning (Figure 21). Study Nast's symbolization of greed and corruption in his graphic symbol of Boss Tweed in "Let Us Prey" (Figure 22). Observe the direct vigor with which a precocious five-year-old used symbol figures to describe the animated interplay between boys and girls (Figure 23).

Project Ten

LEARNING TO SYMBOLIZE: INVENTING SYMBOLIC FORMS

Create one or more of the anthropomorphic (having human attributes) figures suggested below.

1. Combining circles (draw around coins or other small round objects) with dollar signs ($), create a figure entitled "Money Man."

2. Using scribbles that suggest anatomical forms, create a symbol of "Confusion," or "Bewildered Man."

3. Using straight ruled lines, business-machine, algebraic, and related symbols, create "Automation."

4. Place drops of ink on paper and extend them by blowing or spreading them with another piece of paper to create a symbol of "Mr. Rohrschach."

5. Create your own anthropomorphic figure and title it.

part 2

THE ART ELEMENTS

READ Chapter 13, Line, in *Drawing*. Lines that delineate the edges of forms, separating each volume or area from neighboring ones, are termed *contour* lines. In its simplest and most characteristic aspect, the contour line is unvaried in width, is not reinforced by graduated values of shading, and does not seek to describe the modulations of surface within the edges unless they constitute relatively separate forms (Figures 24, 5, 25). At its most expressive the contour line appears to describe the movement of the draftsman's eye as it follows the edges of a form. To develop sensitivity and skill at contour drawing, the draftsman tries to develop an exact and almost unconscious correspondence between the movement of his eye as it searches out the exact indentations and undulations of edge and the movement of his hand holding the pencil or pen. This faculty of eye and hand coordination is most valuable in all drawing activities and for this reason pure contour drawing is of great importance in training draftsmen.

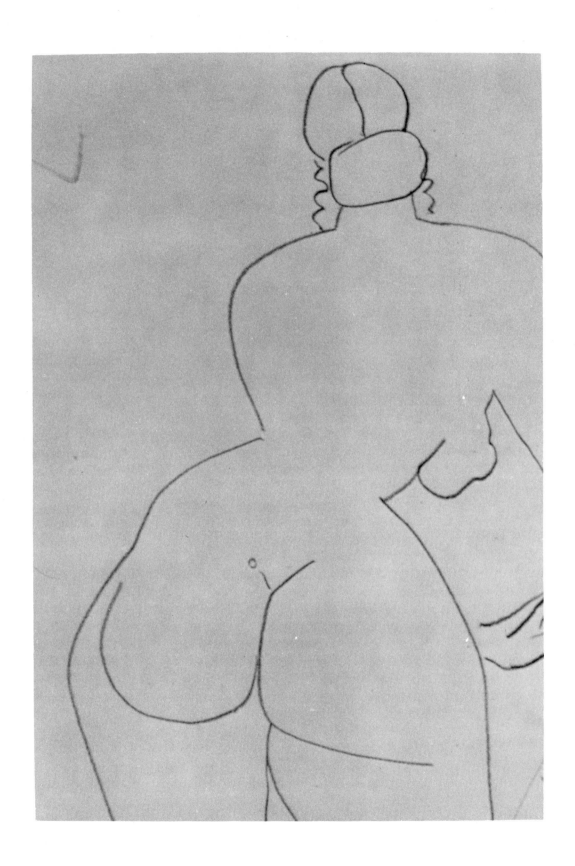

24. *Contour line.*
Detail of "Standing Nude," Gaston Lachaise.
Drawing, *Figure 13–5.*
Whitney Museum of American Art, New York.

The Art Elements: Line

Project Twelve

LINE: THE CONTOUR LINE

A soft pencil is best for beginning contour drawing since it produces a firm, relatively unmodulated line. Place in front of you a solid, nongeometric, irregular form, such as a squash, a not too compact pillow, a hat, a work shoe, or a pitcher's or catcher's glove. Start drawing at some clearly defined point, such as the closest corner of the pillow. If the object you are drawing is not more than 12 or 15 inches across the largest dimension, try to make your drawing about life-size or slightly smaller. Without glancing back at your drawing any more frequently than is *absolutely necessary* to keep your bearings, let your eye move *slowly* along each contour and keep your pencil moving in pace with the movements of your eye. Try to respond to each indentation and bulge of edge with an equivalent hand movement. When you come to a point where the surface you are drawing disappears behind another or flattens out and disappears, stop, look back at your drawing, and commence with the adjoining surface. When your outline is completed, study the drawing in relation to the model and add any internal details that are necessary to make the drawing fully comprehensible. Much of the effectiveness of contour drawing results from its economy. Remember this when adding details. Contour drawings often get wildly out of proportion since the artist is not supposed to look back at the drawing except when absolutely necessary, but this should not discourage beginners since the primary concern is sensitivity of edge rather than accuracy of proportion.

Change the position of your model and repeat the performance. Draw other objects in the same way.

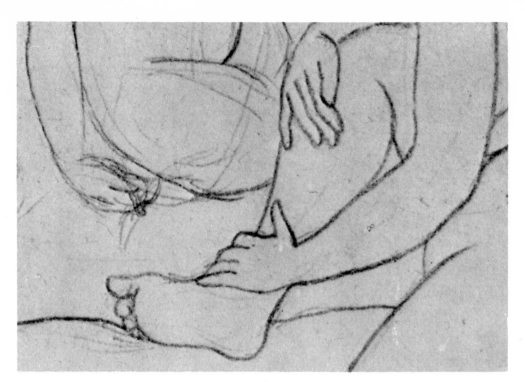

25. *Contour line of varied widths.*
Detail of "The Bathers,"
Pablo Picasso. Drawing, *Figure 10–5.*
Fogg Art Museum, Cambridge, Mass.
(Meta and Paul J. Sachs Collection).

Project Thirteen

LINE: THE CONTOUR LINE

Do a contour drawing of a fairly complex form or group of forms. A basket of vegetables, a paper bag with bananas, oranges, and apples pouring from it, a potted succulent or cactus plant with large fleshy leaves, a still life containing many forms of a not too symmetrical nature. (Bisymmetric objects are not good because beginners are apt to be disturbed by the inevitable sharp deviations from symmetry that occur in contour drawing.) Commence with the closest form or the most forward part. Try to draw all around each form or part without glancing at your hand or drawing. Exaggerate the characterizing aspect of each object or part to achieve a maximum sense of difference.

Whenever possible, do a contour drawing of life models, clothed models, heads or casts of figures or heads. Repeat from various viewpoints. From time to time practice contour drawing in your sketchbook. Establishing the habit of looking at the subject rather than at your drawing, for developing correspondence of eye-hand movement is most important to a draftsman.

A comparison of the contour line used in the Gaston Lachaise drawing of a "Standing Figure" (Figure 24) with Picasso's "Bathers" (Figure 25) reveals much greater sensitivity in the latter. This in-

THE ART ELEMENTS

26. *Amplified contour line.*
Detail of "Head," Pablo Picasso. Drawing, Figure 10–4.
San Francisco Museum of Art (Harriet Lane Levy Bequest).

creased sensitivity results from two factors: first, there is the more analytical examination of form in the Picasso drawings and, secondly, an increasingly expressive quality to the line. This increased sensitivity is to a considerable degree expressed by variations in the widths of line. These changes in width are created by the varying pressures of the hand which represents a response to the importance of a change of direction or an overlapping of forms in much the same way that differing degrees of emphasis in speech reveal the varying values a speaker places upon his words. Sometimes a thicker line also suggests the darker value created by a shadow which by virtue of its darkness makes a strong impact upon the observer's consciousness. In the detail from "The Bathers" (Figure 25) the basis for differing thicknesses of line width can be easily seen. In observing the relationship of thigh and stomach, it is evident that the line describing the thigh is heavier and consequently stands in front of the stomach. The same is true of where the arm rests on the stomach, and one also has the feeling that the increased darkness of line here also describes the slight shadow thrown by the arm. Directly above the elbow the tapered line that describes the division between the stomach and the thorax suggests the gradual diminishing fold of flesh and accompanying shadow. Such changes in line width are not consciously calculated by the artist but represent a spontaneous response to visual and motor stimuli, for the very act of drawing, involving as it does such factors as varying directions of movements or changes of hand position, result in changing line widths. In carrying out the project suggested below there should not be a conscious attempt to change widths of line but rather to vary pressure on the drawing instrument in accordance with the desire to emphasize important edges.

Project Fourteen

LINE: THE CONTOUR LINE OF VARIED WIDTHS

Draw the same subject as in Projects Twelve or Thirteen or a similar one. Use conscious variations of pressure on the pencil to describe overlapping planes, darkness of shadow, or other aspects of form that

27. Clustered lines.
Detail of "A Study for 'The Bathers,' "
Auguste Renoir. Drawing, *Figure 8–7.*
Wadsworth Atheneum, Hartford.

can be implied by changes in the width and darkness of line. Doing such a drawing demands a more continuous reference and cross-reference to the subject of your drawing than did the previous contour drawings. Do not hesitate to look back and forth from drawing to subject as often as you feel necessary but remember that it is better to keep your eyes on the subject than on the drawing.

Project Fifteen

LINE: THE CONTOUR LINE OF VARIED WIDTHS—A FIGURE STUDY

In the manner suggested in Project Fourteen, draw a life model, a clothed model, a head in three-quarter view, or a cast of a human figure or head. Repeat from a variety of views. Do this as frequently as possible.

Throughout the ages artists have felt the need to reinforce pure outline with suggestions of modeling for many subtleties of form are not revealed by the single contour line, even when varying thicknesses of line are used, such as are suggested in Projects Fourteen and Fifteen. Thus a tendency is felt when drawing to amplify gradations of line width with additional lines, graduated values and descriptive textures. A good illustration of this tendency to extend and amplify outline is provided by a "Head" by Picasso (Figure 26). Here the outline often breaks its movement and changes direction to suggest overlapping planes at the edge of the form. Occasionally this broken line is amplified by additional strokes, most noticeably in the nose, thereby suggesting complexities of form beyond the implications of the single outline.

An extension of this amplified line is provided by a detail from Renoir's "Bathers" (Figure 27). Here the outline is made up of loosely applied lines which parallel the edges of the form in an easy flowing rhythm, thus at the same time enriching the sense of three dimensions, suggesting the movements of the bathing figure and the relaxed and joyous act of drawing.

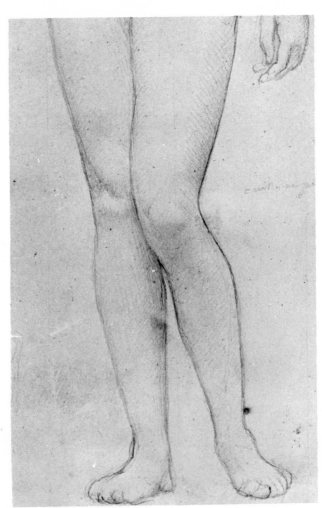

28. *Modeled outline.*
Detail of Two Nudes,
Study for the "Golden Age,"
Jean-Auguste Dominique Ingres.
Drawing, *Figure 7–1.*
Fogg Museum of Art, Cambridge, Mass.
(Grenville Lindall Winthrop Collection).

A detail from Ingres' Two Nudes, Study for the "Golden Age" (Figure 28) departs farther from outline by using a technique related to the Renaissance discipline of drawing. This is beautifully illustrated along the girl's thigh where a series of fine pencil lines which seem to follow the surface of the form gradually coalesce with the outlines to increase the sense of solid form.

Project Sixteen

LINE: THE DELINEATING EDGE—THE BROKEN LINE AND REPEATED LINE

Select as a subject a solid form with contours of considerable complexity, such as a cabbage with several leaves curled back from the main mass, a branch with large leaves which have undulating edges, a catcher's glove, the cast of a head, or a human head. If you have a large mirror and good light, you might attempt a self-portrait. Using a pencil, and drawing a little less than life-size, use a slightly broken line such as you see in the Picasso head. When an edge seems ambiguous and you have difficulty defining it, see if two or three lines seem more adequate.

Project Seventeen

LINE: THE DELINEATING EDGE—LINEAR CLUSTERS

Using the same subject as in the previous project or one of the others suggested for it, employ such freely flowing lines as those in the Renoir drawing. Make the lines with easy movements of your hand so that they are not rigidly parallel to one another or the edge of the form. Be certain to observe the form carefully as you draw, and you will find that your perception of roundness, flatness, and convergence of surfaces as they approach the contours will determine the spread or convergence of the clustered contour lines. Remember that the primary purpose of these bundles of lines is to describe the forms within the mass as fully as possible along the boundaries.

Project Eighteen

LINE: THE DELINEATING EDGE—THE MODELED LINE

Use of any of the subjects suggested in Project Sixteen. Shade the form near the contour with light groups of parallel lines which curve according to the directions the form seems to take. Study the edges carefully and modify the curvature of the lines of shading in any way that seems to describe the form more fully. If the curved lines of shading separate from the outlines and the two seem unrelated, see if lines drawn parallel to the edges of the form and merging into the outline will bind them together.

Draw as many objects as you can using the previous suggestions for amplifying outlines in any combination that helps describe the form you are observing. Do not try to describe light and shadow but merely use supplementary lines, tones, and textures to reinforce the contours and thereby create a fuller sense of form than can be achieved by pure outline.

29. *Calligraphic line.*
Detail from a "Sketchbook Page,"
Jean Louis Forain. Drawing,
Figure 1–7. Art Institute of Chicago
(Gift of Frank B. Hubachek).

■ *The Calligraphic Line*

In drawing, line not only has a descriptive function but also an expressive function. We have seen how variations of thick and thin describe perceptions of form, overlapping edges and light and shadow. Variations of line width also relate to the gesture by which a line is made, so that a sweeping stroke, made rapidly, commenced while the hand is in motion in the air and finished by lifting the hand, usually creates a tapered line that describes the action by which the line was created. While the creation of such a line sounds self-conscious, in the work of an experienced and excited draftsman the gestures are far from deliberate but result naturally from the action of drawing. A glance at the figure of a man from a page in Forain's "Sketchbook" (Figure 29) reveals the kind of tapered lines that suggest a hand in motion, starting with a light moving touch, bearing down more heavily in the main part of the line, and then lifting.

The character of a tapered line results from the medium used as well as the gesture of execution, for the medium to a degree determines the gesture. A pointed brush and ink provide for wide variations of line width, as can be seen in a detail from the drawing of "Mother and Child" by Rivera (Figure 9). A flexible pen creates a lively and expressive effect (Figure 90). Pencil, charcoal, and chalk also respond to differing emphasis and reflect the movement of the hand in variations of both width and value, for in using the dry media as one presses down the line becomes darker.

Project Nineteen

LINE: THE CALLIGRAPHIC LINE—VARYING LINE WIDTHS

Throughout this project practice using (1) a well-sharpened pencil held between the thumb and the first two fingers of the hand, (2) a one-inch piece of charcoal held in the same way. To do this, pick up the pencil or charcoal as if you were extracting a thumbtack. This position allows for much more variation in the amount of contact between medium and paper than occurs in the conventional writing position and thus encourages a greater latitude in line width.

Keeping arm and wrist relaxed, make free swinging movements of the hand describing wavy lines, spirals and gently curved shapes. Hold the pencil so that the pressure varies from being on the point to being on the side as this creates a line that varies from thin to wide. The charcoal will provide even greater variations of line width. When you hold the piece of charcoal parallel to the direction of your line, it will make a narrow mark; as you move the charcoal at right angles to the direction in which the line moves, the line will increase in width. Since the charcoal is used in making relatively large drawings, use sweeping movements of the arm so that your lines cover an entire sheet of newsprint. On a full sheet of newsprint make rapid large drawings of simple objects, using pencil and charcoal, working for a wide variety of line widths.

With a brush dipped in ink, draw a freely curved line. Commence

30. *Linear calligraphy by a Japanese master*. Detail of "The Mochi Makers," Hokusai. Drawing, *Figure 9–9*. Metropolitan Museum of Art, New York (Gift in memory of Charles Stewart Smith, 1914).

the line in the air, then allow the brush to gradually touch the paper, and finally lift the brush as you complete the line. This should produce a gracefully tapered line. After an initial period of practice sufficient so that you feel you have some control of the lines, copy the lines in the body of Forain's "Man" (Figure 29) or the detail from Rivera's "Mother and Child," *Drawing* (Figure 9). In copying these do not try for any exact duplication but rather aim for flexibility of line and free execution.

Project Twenty

LINE: CALLIGRAPHIC LINE—SIMPLE OBJECTS

Execute this project in (1) either pencil or charcoal or both, and (2) brush and ink. Select a simple subject with undulating contours, a wide-brimmed hat, a man's old hiking boot or work shoe, a cluster of large leaves, a potted succulent or cactus, a few large vegetables.

31. *Calligraphic line by a modern master. Detail of "Seated Clown," Rico Lebrun. Drawing, Figure 13–14.* Santa Barbara Museum of Art.

Draw them freely, trying for definite variations in line width that seem to grow from the act of drawing. Keep your drawing sufficiently large so that your gestures can be free and not constricted. Since drawings of this type can be executed quite rapidly, repeat the project a number of times and finally select and keep the drawing in each medium which you think has the most authority to its linear character.

Project Twenty-one

LINE: THE CALLIGRAPHIC LINE

Calligraphy is defined as "beautiful writing" and when the beauty of line that results from the flourish of execution becomes a major esthetic aim, we have the true calligraphic line. Study the details from "The Mochi Makers," by Hokusai (Figure 30), "Seated Clown," by Lebrun (Figure 31), and Rembrandt's "Winter Landscape" (Figure 32)—three splendid examples of calligraphic virtuosity discussed in *Drawing*. Each of these masterpieces of draftsmanship draws upon the lifetime of experience necessary to achieve a personal style, mature in its assured execution. The beginner cannot hope to do more than become aware of the factors involved. Select one of the previously executed subjects and sketch it lightly in pencil so that you can concentrate upon the execution rather than upon problems of size, shape, and relationship of parts. Proceed with brush and ink using variations of pressure to correspond either to the relationships of form you see or that grow naturally from the act of drawing. Do not try to follow your pencil lines exactly for this will tend to inhibit

THE ART ELEMENTS

32. *Calligraphic line
by a European master. Detail of
"Winter Landscape,"
Rembrandt van Rijn.*
Drawing, *Figure 5–13.* Courtesy of the
Fogg Art Museum, Cambridge, Mass.
(Charles A. Loeser Bequest).

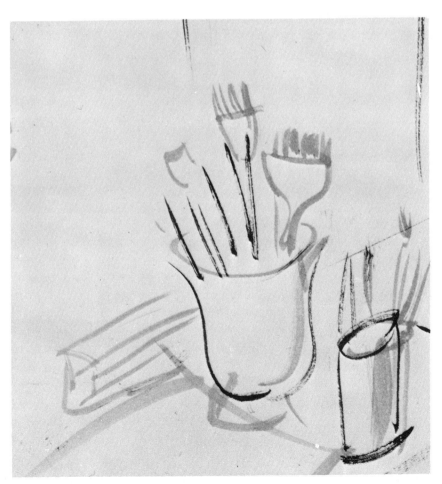

33. *The lyric line.
Detail from "The Artist's Studio,"
Raoul Dufy. Drawing, Figure 10–2.*
Museum of Modern Art, New York
(Gift of Mr. and Mrs. Peter A. Rübel).

34. *The emphatic line.*
Detail of "The Bridge
at L'Anglois." Vincent van Gogh.
Drawing, *Figure 15–2.*
Los Angeles County Museum of Art
(The Mr. and Mrs. George Gard De
Sylva Fund).

the freedom of your strokes. Do not try to imitate any of the efforts
you see in the calligraphic drawings you have studied but try to
produce a drawing that expresses (1) the character of the subject,
(2) the nature of brush and ink, (3) the act of drawing. As you
develop assurance of performance and an appreciation of characterful rendering, your own personal calligraphy will emerge.

In discussing line, Chapter 1 of *Drawing* states: "The simplest
line suggests direction, divides space, has length, width, tone, texture,
and may suggest contour. As soon as the line begins to change direction, to move in a curved or angular fashion, to fluctuate in width
and to have rough or smooth edges, its active and descriptive power is
increased many times. The beginning student, learning to draw, soon
discovers he is assuming command over a most powerful tool. With
it he can describe, suggest, evoke, and imply an endless variety of
experiences, observations, conceptions, and intuitions. Every mark
one makes, whether a thoughtful line or a careless scribble, will inevitably convey something of the maker to the sensitive observer."
The projects dealing with line have been designed to make the beginner aware of the functions of line. The following exercises are
planned to provide some initial explorations in the expressive quali-

35. *The flowing line.*
Detail of "Odalisque,"
Henri Matisse.
Drawing,
Figure 10–1. Achenbach
Foundation for Graphic Arts,
California Palace of the
Legion of Honor, San
Francisco (Gift of Frank
Schwabacher, Jr.).

ties of line. It is important to realize that an artist does not consciously use a certain type of line to express a particular attitude. Both the attitude and character of line are inherent in the artist's artistic temperament, so much so that he need not be conscious of certain attitudes to express them. But self-discovery is most important. This occurs, not on a conscious and verbal level, but rather when the artist finds ways of working that are satisfying, comfortable, exhilarating and right for him. The next projects in line provide initial exploration with the hope that some of the suggested ways of working may "feel right" and provide a starting point for self-discovery.

36. *The crabbed line.*
Detail of "Workmen and Cripple,"
George Grosz. Drawing,
Figure 11–7. Richard Feigen
Gallery, Inc., Chicago.

Project Twenty-two

LINE: EXPERIENCING DIFFERENT LINE QUALITIES

In the last section of Chapter 13 in *Drawing*, the expressive character of various line movements are categorized as the lyric line, the emphatic line, the flowing line, the crabbed line, the meandering line, and the encompassing line (Figures 8, 33, 34, 35, 36, 37). Using pencil, doodle freely using the kinds of line movements observed in the various illustrations in *Drawing* between pages 307 and 313. You may feel the character of the line more sharply if you copy small sections of drawings, but do this freely, avoiding a cramped self-conscious copying of your model. Accuracy is not as important as getting the "feel" of the way of working. If you like certain kinds of line movement or they seem to come naturally to your hand movements, do drawings in that particular manner. Try to select subject matter that appears appropriate to each way of working: For instance, (1) you might find the lyric line appropriate for a pencil drawing of one of the following subjects: a still life of a bouquet of flowers, a drawing of a Rococo figurine, an imaginative or symbolic visualization of an amusement park, a mountain stream, or child's play. (2) The emphatic line might seem better suited to a charcoal or brush and ink drawing of a man's work shoe, a stratified rock, or a section of cordwood. The same media and type of line might intensify an imaginative expression titled "Nightmare" or a symbol of "Explosion." (3) The flowing line conforms naturally to such subjects as reflections in quiet water or the rendering of any *Art-Nouveau* concept. (4) The meandering line suggests either erratic movements, the flight of a butterfly for instance, or contorted, tight, and nervous emphasis, such as one might desire if visualizing a theme involving tension or conflict, describing the uncertain gait of a drunkard or drawing a dry, desiccated, or thorny bush. (5) The continuous circular movements of hand involving the encompassing line are best suited for drawing voluminous objects and rounded forms like corpulent human figures, large pumpkins, or billowing clouds. The visualization of objects to be modeled in clay or any other weighty plastic

THE ART ELEMENTS

37. *The meandering line. Detail of "Portrait of Madame Vuillard," Jean Édouard Vuillard. Drawing, Figure 13–16. Yale University Art Gallery, New Haven, Conn.*

material might also be projected with a strong sense of bulk by using the encompassing line. Whenever you commence drawing an object or idea, think about the kind of line that seems equally right for you and for the subject.

■ Form and Value

Read Chapter 14, Form and Value, in *Drawing*. Some of the concepts presented in this chapter have already been touched on, for all aspects of drawing are interrelated. Just as the complexities of language are such that in learning to write one can profit from dissecting the sentence to study the parts of grammar separately, so in drawing, the interrelationships of parts to the whole can best be perceived by becoming aware of the various elements and developing resourcefulness in their manipulation.

The use of black, white, and the intervening grays (or any monochro-

38. *Diagonal pencil lines used for gray values.*
Detail of "Seated Woman," Guiseppe Bernardino Bison.
Drawing, *Figure 4–12.* Collection of Dr. Robert Prentice.

matic color scheme, in fact) is, like line, a convention that does not exist in nature but one we accept in drawing. Learning to use black, white, and the intervening grays which make up the value scale will provide material for the next projects.

Project Twenty-three

FORM AND VALUE: THE VALUE SCALE

Note: For the projects using charcoal, one may wish to add white charcoal paper to the list of materials. Charcoal paper has a more interesting texture than newsprint, is more durable, and so permits a more finished drawing.

The traditional way of making grays of varying value with pencil is to use a series of parallel lines moving either vertically, horizontally, or diagonally. The latter is used most frequently because it comes more naturally to the movements of the hand and with slight modifications of direction suggests the surface movement of three-dimensional forms (Figure 38).

1. Using any system for making a gray by combining pencil lines, make a graduated strip about 2 inches wide and 6 inches long, shading from very light gray to the darkest shade possible. (Since graphite is not black you cannot get as dark gray with pencil as with charcoal or ink.)

2. Scribbled line movements (Figure 8) or a formalized texture pattern (Figure 39) are appealing to certain temperaments and esthetic purposes. Create another value gradation using a very different system than was employed in your first one.

3. Using a larger strip (about 3 inches wide and 8 inches high is a good size for all of the charcoal exercises) make a value gradation with charcoal without rubbing to fuse lines. (Figure 40).

4. A value gradation with a less linear texture can be made by building the gradations of darkness through repeated applications, using the side of a short piece of charcoal. A gentle rotary movement usu-

39. *Pencil used in formalized texture-pattern for gray values.*
Detail of "Port," Albert Gleizes. Drawing, Figure 16–12.
Solomon R. Guggenheim Museum.

40. *Value gradations built up in charcoal without rubbing to fuse lines. Detail of "I Know Not Why," R. Baxter. Drawing, Figure 16–4. Collection of the artist.*

41. *Academic drawing. Repeated applications of charcoal fused by rubbing. "Still Life of Casts," G. A. Frost. 14″ x 21″. Collection of the author.*

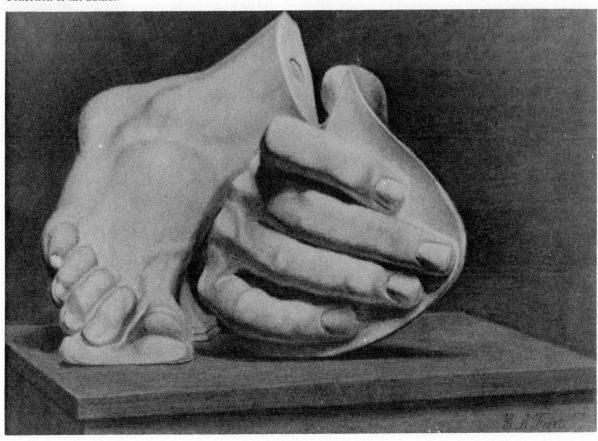

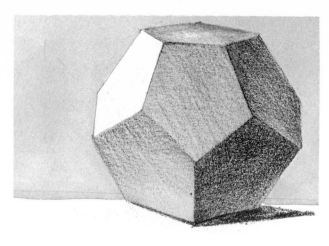

42. *Illuminated polyhedron*
with value planes suggesting form.
Drawing, *Figure 14–2.*

ally creates an even texture. Build a value gradation using this technique but do not try to contain the rectangle within sharp outlines.

5. The traditional French Beaux-Arts academic training stressed the use of charcoal to build delicate gradations of value in which almost all suggestion of the method of application was carefully obscured (Figure 41). "In making such drawings the charcoal stick was carefully pointed by rubbing it on sandpaper, and then even gray values were built up with lightly applied parallel lines. Each set of parallel lines was then rubbed with a paper stump, reinforced with another set of lines, rubbed, and this was repeated until tones of the desired smoothness were established." Using either a paper stump or tortillon (or if these are difficult to procure, a rolled piece of paper or paper-toweling works well), build up a smooth gradation from white to black.

Project Twenty-four

FORM AND VALUE: FORM

Place a white or very light colored geometric form (a cube or better yet a polygonal form) so that it receives a strong light from above and to one side. Using any one of the techniques practiced in Project Twenty-three, The Value Scale, build up gradations of value, leaving the white paper for the lightest surface and using the darkest value you can create for the deepest shadow, which might well be the cast shadow (Figure 42). If you do not have access to white geometric forms, a cardboard carton with the open flaps propped at interesting angles, or a covered cardboard box such as a stationary box with the cover removed and leaned against the bottom at an interesting angle provides an excellent substitute. Observe your geometric object and the cast shadows carefully. Draw the objects as large as is practical for the medium you are using. (Students have a tendency to draw too small, partly a hangover from elementary and high school paper sizes, partly because smallness seems easier to encompass.) A pencil drawing is too big when it is difficult to build values of even texture, a charcoal drawing is too small when the stick of charcoal seems clumsily oversize.

THE ART ELEMENTS

43. *The elements of traditional chiaroscuro.*

highlight
light
shadow
core of shadow
reflected light
cast shadow

Project Twenty-five

FORM AND VALUE: CHIAROSCURO AND FORM

In the systematic chiaroscuro traditionally used to describe form, the following elements were employed: (1) light, (2) highlight, (3) shadow, (4) core of shadow, (5) reflected light, and (6) cast shadow (Figure 43). Place a sphere, preferably white, although any light color will do, under strong light. Study the form carefully before you commence to draw, observing the way in which the shadow becomes intensified as the surface of the sphere moves away from the source of light. Also look for the reflected lights which are cast into the shadow areas from illuminated nearby surfaces. If the sphere is not shiny there will be no highlights. Proceed with your drawing, using the method you prefer to build the dark values. If you use a light, even tone of gray for your background, the sense of brilliant illumination will be intensified.

Project Twenty-six

FORM AND VALUE: COMPLEX FORMS

Compose a still-life arrangement containing large, rather simple forms (Figure 41). (If the objects are all of closely related values, preferably light in color, the use of chiaroscuro to describe form will not be complicated by differences of color.) A still life of kitchen bowls, potatoes, and squashes, or of apples and oranges works well. Simple vase forms, two or three inflated beach balls or floating toys, a plaster cast, or a group of plaster casts provide good subjects. Sketch the objects in light outline to insure satisfying size and shape relationships and proceed to develop the forms in dark and light. Study the shapes of cast shadows very carefully and model them as thoughtfully as you do the actual objects. (Beginners often weaken their drawings by concentrating on things. To the mature artist, all aspects of the visual experience are significant: the shadows cast by objects provide elements of pattern equal in importance to the objects.) Place a simple background behind the still life, preferably close enough so that shadows cast by the still life fall on the background and the background surfaces cast reflected lights back into the shadows of the still life.

■ *Form and Value: Sketchbook*

Sketch with masses of dark and light (Figure 44) to convey *light* and *shadow*. Try blocking in the shadow shapes without any preliminary contour lines (Figure 45). Continuous practice of this type of drawing develops a kind of shorthand for indicating form and also builds a strong sense of pattern.

The use of chiaroscuro is only one of many systems that have been devised for conveying form. Among the many schemes that have been evolved over the ages are the various perspective systems and certain diagrammatic methods for indicating structure. Certain of these diagrammatic systems will be discussed first. In the sixteenth century an Italian, Cambiaso, frequently drew the human figure with bold simplifications that reduced its rounded organic forms to blocks, pyramidal and tapered rectangles, and other geometric forms (Figure 46). Cambiaso reinforced his simplifications of form with an equally simplified version of chiaroscuro.

The most influential diagrammatic method developed in modern times to indicate form was that used by Cézanne in his drawings and paintings. A detail from his "Study from Houdon's 'Écorché'" (Figure 47) reveals the method with particular clarity. Cézanne felt that, to convey the facts of form as he perceived them, it was necessary to simplify nature's complexities into somewhat geometric components, but the simplifications are less arbitrary and more subtle than those employed by Cambiaso. As can be seen in the "Écorché," human anatomy has been translated into spherical, cylindrical, and conical elements in interpenetrating relationships. So that the system would not seem too rigid and static, clusters of lines were used to define areas.

Project Twenty-seven

FORM AND VALUE: SCHEMATIC FORM

Use a cast of the human figure, a cast of a head, or a life model. If none of these subjects are available, you might attempt a self-portrait. Have your subject well lighted from one side so that the planes of the form are clearly defined. Using firm outlines translate the complexities of your subject into geometric forms defined by flat planes à la Cambiaso. To strengthen and clarify form relationships, shade the under planes and those on the side away from the light. In this and the following projects use pencil or charcoal and draw freely on a full sheet of newsprint.

Project Twenty-eight

FORM AND VALUE: SCHEMATIC FORM

If available, draw an "Écorché" (plaster cast showing the muscles of a human figure), otherwise again draw from one of the subjects suggested for Project Twenty-seven. Try to define the elements of the form in a manner similar to that employed in Cézanne's study (Figure 47). This can best be accomplished by a somewhat free and intuitive analysis of form. Work freely, trusting your eyes and hand rather than attempting a too stringent, intellectual (verbal) analysis. (The verbal orientation toward which we tend because of our basically verbal education is revealed by the fact that *intellectual* means verbal in preference to visual for most people.)

Project Twenty-nine

FORM AND VALUE: SCHEMATIC FORM

Set up a still life containing objects with clearly structured forms, such as segmented vegetables (pumpkins or squash), large bones or shells. A partially crunched large paper bag provides a good form for this problem. Stratified rocks or large mineral specimens also work well. Use a diagrammatic sketching style to indicate the forms and the interrelationships of parts. Your problem is to simplify and clarify by delineating basic forms that will reveal structural relationships. Certain very visually minded students will find this exercise too foreign to their temperament to have value. Those with a tendency to abstract will enjoy and profit from translating nature's organic complexities into formally structured equivalents. The chief function of these three last projects is to help students see form.

■ Perspective: Forms in Space

We were introduced to perspective on pages 12–18 when we carried out some simple exercises involving overlapping forms, diminishing sizes, layered space and isometric perspective. Perspective is the traditional device used in Western art to suggest space by systematically diminishing the sizes of objects and foreshortening the shapes of parts as they recede into the distance. The theory of perspective is based upon certain premises. First, that the eye of the observer is in a fixed position. Secondly, that the surface of the paper upon which the drawing is done constitutes a plane of vision. The term *plane of vision* may need explanation. If you look straight in front of you through a pane of glass that is parallel to the front of your face, this pane of glass represents a plane of vision. If you were to draw on this pane of glass, delineating the edges of objects seen through the glass without moving your head, this act would correspond to doing a perspective drawing. The piece of paper upon which you ordinarily draw corresponds to the pane of glass and constitutes the plane of vision.

One simple and fundamental concept relates all the complexities of perspective: that objects appear to diminish in size as they recede into the distance. This diminishing persists until, given enough unobstructed space, all objects disappear. This illusion of shrinking with distance occurs with absolute regularity so that a series of objects of uniform size, such as telephone poles, placed equidistant and in a straight line on a flat plane, moving into space, appear progressively smaller in a mathematically determinable progression, as do all of their parts and the distances between them. It follows, then, that a plane of uniform height and width diminishes in its height and width

as it goes into the distance to vanish at a point called the *vanishing point*. We generalize about this by saying that sets of parallel lines (the edges of a real or theoretical plane of uniform width) converge to a vanishing point as they go into the distance. This phenomenon is easily observed in railway tracks, highways, or when regularly shaped and spaced objects extend in front of one into deep space. The vanishing points at which parallel lines meet in the distance always occur on a line that is level with the viewer's eyes. This is called the *horizon line* and the horizon line corresponds to the actual *eye level* of the observer.

While the phenomena of vanishing points and horizon lines can be observed with comparative ease in a few situations, such as when a road, railway tracks, or telephone poles cross a vast flat plane in a straight line, such situations are relatively rare. Usually one is confronted with much more complex interrelationships of form which are much more difficult for the eye (and mind) to assess. The following exercises deal with very simple forms and are planned to illustrate perspective concepts, such as vanishing points, horizon lines, and foreshortened planes as involved in sketching procedures.

44. Sketch with massed darks and lights. Detail of "Study for Manhattan Bridge Loop," (No. 2), Edward Hopper. Drawing, Figure 14–21. Addison Gallery of American Art, Andover, Mass.

Project Thirty

PERSPECTIVE: THE PICTURE PLANE

Place a piece of transparent tracing paper on a pane of window glass and draw around the outlines of some object seen through the glass which presents elements of perspective and foreshortening. An auto-

mobile or house is ideal. Keep your head in one position and do not modify the distance of your head from the glass. Remove the paper from the window and study the results; identify the elements of perspective and foreshortening that are evident. If possible, repeat this performance, drawing the same object from another viewpoint.

Project Thirty-one

PERSPECTIVE: EYE LEVELS, HORIZON LINES, AND VANISHING POINTS

Study Figure 48 and decide what each drawing implies as to the position of the viewer in relation to the cube.

If you have observed the drawings carefully and analyzed the full implications of their varying shapes, you may come to the following conclusions. First, all of the cubes have been sketched from directly in front of the forward corner since you see an equal amount of each side of each cube. Cube number 1 implies that the viewer is either below the cube since the bottom of the cube is visible, or the cube is tilted so that the bottom can be seen. Cube number 2 implies that

THE ART ELEMENTS

46. Organic forms simplified
into geometric components. Detail of
"Tumbling Men," Luca Cambiaso.
Drawing, Figure 18–14.
Uffizi Gallery, Florence.

47. Schematic simplifications of
anatomy. Detail of "Study after Houdon's 'Écorché,'"
Paul Cézanne. Drawing, Figure 13–12.
Metropolitan Museum of Art,
New York (Maria DeWitt Jesup Fund,
1951, from the Museum of Modern Art
Lizzie P. Bliss Collection).

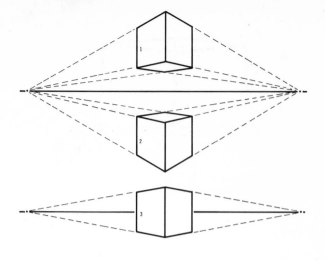

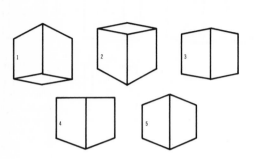

48. *Five cubes seen from varying eye levels.*

the viewer is above the cube and is the same distance above the cube that he was below the cube in number 1 since the same amount of top is visible in 2 as bottom in 1. (If the cube in number 2 is tilted, it is tilted in the opposite direction to cube number 1.) Cube number 3 suggests that the viewer's eyes are half way between the top and bottom of the cube since one can see neither top nor bottom and the perspective of both top and bottom lines is equally acute. In cube number 4 the viewer's eyes are level with the top of the cube since the two receding edges form a straight line. Cube number 5 suggests, as does cube number 3, that the eyes of the viewer are half way between the top and bottom of the cube, but since the perspective is more acute (the angles sharper) than in cube number 3 it appears that the viewer is much closer to the cube.

One arrives at these conclusions without formal knowledge of perspective. General familiarity with perspective drawing enables the viewer to interpret the drawings according to the intent of the draftsman. However, an analysis of the theoretical basis for these drawings provides an insight into the workings of perspective. Figure 49 reveals the perspective concepts implicit in cubes 1, 2 and 3, in Figure 48. These conceptions are: (1) Since objects diminish in size in exact ratio to their distance from the viewer, planes of uniform width (whose edges therefore constitute parallel lines) diminish in width as they go into the distance to disappear at a *vanishing point*. (2) These vanishing points are located on a horizon line that corresponds to the eye level of the observer. If we now study the drawings of Figure 49, we see that with cube number 1 the horizon line is below the cube (since the viewer's eyes are below the cube). Cube number 2 shows the horizon line to be above the cube, and the same distance above that it is below the cube in drawing number 1. In cube number 3 the horizon line is located between the top and bottom of the cube, as was implied by the fact that one could see neither the top nor bottom of the cube.

Draw a sequence of cubes on various levels in heavy pencil lines. With light lines project the perspective of the cubes to vanishing points. Also indicate the horizon lines with light lines.

THE ART ELEMENTS

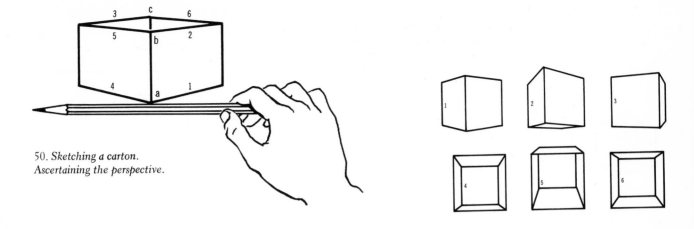

50. *Sketching a carton.*
Ascertaining the perspective.

51. *Six cubes viewed from different positions.*

Project Thirty-two

PERSPECTIVE: DRAW A CARTON

Place an open squarish cardboard carton at least 12 inches wide, at a series of various levels before you—on the floor, on a low table, at your eye level, and considerably above your eye level (to do the last, it is frequently easiest to thumbtack the empty carton to the wall). Keep the forward corner of the carton directly in front of you to minimize complexities of perspective. Observe the varying shapes of the open top and the diminishing amounts of interior evident as the box approaches eye level. As the box gets above eye level notice how an increased area of bottom becomes visible. Sketch the box with an easy free outline in the different positions. If you have difficulty ascertaining the perspective angle, hold your pencil in a horizontal position and allow the pencil to touch point "a" (Figure 50). You can then judge the angles of perspective more objectively. The same procedure can be followed in relation to point "b" and "c," except with point "c" the pencil should be placed above the corner being observed. If your sketches are accurate you can extend lines 1, 2 and 3 in each sketch and discover the vanishing point (and the horizon line) for the right-hand side of the carton, while extending 4, 5, and 6 will give you the vanishing point for the left-hand side of the carton. When sketching free-hand one seldom achieves sufficient accuracy so that the projected lines meet at an exact point, and in such cases the horizon line derived from the vanishing points is seldom a true horizontal. This is relatively easy to correct, and as you develop sketching facility your eye will tend to pick out gross inaccuracies.

After sketching the cartons, try drawing a series of essentially rectangular forms ranging in size through furniture (a chest, table, desk) to buildings. Study your sketches carefully to ascertain whether your drawings suggest the correct eye-level relationship between you and the sketched objects. Very frequently beginners sketch all objects in bird's-eye perspective, that is, as though the artist were above and looking down on them. Remember that if you are draw-

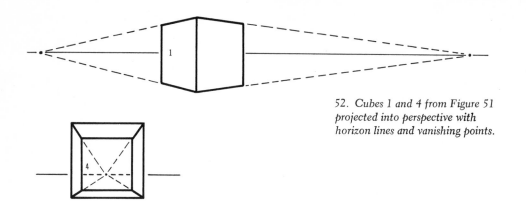

52. *Cubes 1 and 4 from Figure 51 projected into perspective with horizon lines and vanishing points.*

ing an object the top of which is above your eyes, the horizon line on which the vanishing points are located will be below the top of the object.

In all sketching procedures it is desirable to develop visual sensitivity and place a minimum reliance on theoretical procedures and mechanical aids. Thus, vanishing points and the use of the pencil as a plumb line should only be used as a check on accuracy or to dispel acute confusion.

Project Thirty-three

PERSPECTIVE: ONE- AND TWO-POINT PERSPECTIVE

Figure 51 presents another series of cubes. Study them and again decide what the full implications are as to the position of the viewer in relation to the cubes.

The implications of the six drawings that make up Figure 51 are as follows: In 1 the viewer stands slightly to the left of the front corner of the cube and consequently sees more of the right side than of the left. His eye level is about in the middle of the cube so the bottom edges rise toward the horizon line at the same angle that the top edges descend. In 2 the viewer still stands to the left of the corner of the cube but is close to the corner and consequently sees more of the right and less of the left side of the cube. The eye level is slightly below the bottom of the cube. In 3 the viewer stands slightly to the right of the cube and closer to the corner than in either cube 1 or 2 and consequently sees less of the right and more of the left-hand side. Because he is closer to the corner than in either of the other two sketches, he sees less of the side which is in acute perspective than in either of the previous sketches. The eye level is between the bottom and top of the cube but closer to the bottom than to the top; consequently, the perspective lines of the bottom slant up at a lesser angle than the top lines slant down. Number 4. Here one appears to be directly in front looking into an open cube. The eye level is about one

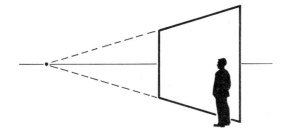

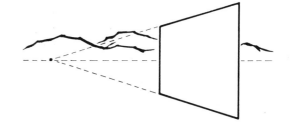

54. *The perspective horizon line
determined by eye level and the actual
horizon are seldom identical.*

third up from the bottom of the cube. In 5 one is still looking into the cube from directly in front but the eye level is slightly above the top of the cube. In 6 one is still directly in front of the cube with the eye level about a third from the top of the cube.

Now place a piece of tracing paper over each of the cubes, trace the cubes and continue the lines of the sides until they meet at common vanishing points. Use heavy lines to outline the cubes and light lines for the perspective and horizon lines, as in Figure 52. You will notice that cubes 1, 2, and 3 have two vanishing points each, while 4, 5, and 6 have only one vanishing point for each cube. This can be explained as follows: Each set of parallel lines one sees receding into the distance has its own vanishing point. In the sketches of cubes 1, 2, and 3 the two visible sides of the cubes are at right angles to each other, consequently present two separate sets of parallel lines, and so require two vanishing points. Since cubes 4, 5, and 6 are directly in front of the viewer, all of the edges of the receding interior planes are parallel so the four lines which describe these edges meet at a common vanishing point. (1) Draw a series of solid cubes as though you were standing to the left, the right, high above the cube, or below it. Project the perspective of the cubes to the horizon lines, as in Figure 52, then correct the drawing of the cubes until the projected lines meet at vanishing points on a horizontal horizon line. (2) Assume a series of open cubes have been placed directly before you. Draw them as though they were in varying degrees below and above your eye level. Project the perspective, and if the lines do not meet at one central vanishing point, make the necessary corrections.

Project Thirty-four

PERSPECTIVE: THE HORIZON LINE

We have found that the horizon line upon which vanishing points are placed is at eye level. Eye level means the *actual height* of the eyes of the viewer-artist in relation to the object being drawn. If an artist is drawing an eleven-foot-high wall which stands on a piece of ground level with the artist and the artist's eyes are five and one-half

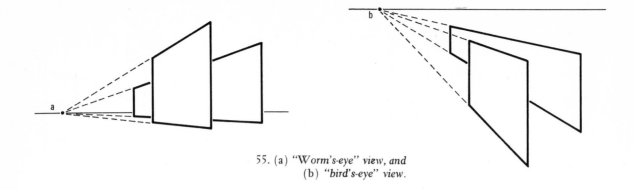

55. (a) "Worm's-eye" view, and
    (b) "bird's-eye" view.

feet above the ground, the horizon line will be in the middle of the wall and the lines which define the top and bottom of the wall will converge at exactly the same angle. This can be seen in Figure 53.

When one is sketching out-of-doors the theoretical horizon line which corresponds to eye level seldom corresponds to the actual horizon line. The theoretical horizon line is based on the concept of an absolutely flat plane extending as far as one can see, and this seldom occurs in nature except when one is confronted by a vast body of water such as the ocean. As a consequence when one is sketching out-of-doors one usually constructs a theoretical horizon line by observing the perspective in the buildings being drawn rather than trying to place vanishing points on the actual horizon. In drawing a wall, such as depicted in Figure 53, the actual horizon might well look like Figure 54.

Draw around this book to provide a frame for the following exercise. In an imaginary landscape setting similar to Figure 55 draw a series of walls running into the distance. Assume a constant eye level and include one wall which is half the height of your eye level, one equal to your eye level, one twice your eye level. Add walls of other heights and place fence posts, telephone poles, and other objects in the landscape. Place distant hills, such as you see in Figure 54, to suggest the landscape setting. Remember that the bottom of walls and objects cannot be placed arbitrarily. If, as in Figure 53, an eleven-foot wall extends an equal amount below and above the horizon line, a twenty-two-foot-high wall would be placed one-fourth below and three-fourths above the horizon line. This same proportion will maintain no matter where in the composition the wall is placed. For instance, the top of a five-and-a-half-foot object will always be at the horizon line.

Project Thirty-five

PERSPECTIVE: LOW AND HIGH HORIZON LINES

As stated before, eye level, consequently horizon line, is determined by the actual level of the viewer-artist in relation to the object being

56. *An infinite number of lines can be projected to one vanishing point provided they are parallel to one another.*

drawn. If the wall in Figure 53 were viewed from an eminence far above the height of the wall the eye level, horizon line, and vanishing points would be raised correspondingly and the effect would be as in Figure 55b. If the same wall were viewed from a seated position so the eye level were two and three-fourths feet from the ground, the eye level, horizon line, and vanishing points would be lowered as in Figure 55a. A high eye level provides what is frequently described as a "bird's-eye" view, a low eye level a "worm's-eye" view.

Draw the same group of walls and objects as in Project Fifty-five from a bird's-eye view. Repeat from a worm's-eye view.

An infinite number of sets of parallel lines can meet at one vanishing point as can be seen in Figure 56. Here warehouses, loading platforms, doors, windows, tracks, and so on, all rectangular forms which parallel one another, are at right angles to the picture plane (the front façade of the buildings are parallel to the artist's face), and so go into perspective to a common vanishing point in the center of the picture. The same phenomenon can be observed in Leonardo's perspective study for the "Adoration of the Magi" (Figure 57) and in Gondolfo's "Figures and Animals in Deep Perspective View" (Figure 58).

Project a complex grouping of rectangular structures into one-point perspective. Any long corridor such as one sees in the average school, with doorways opening from it, lockers lining the walls, and so on provides such a problem. If you have access to such a subject, draw it from a central position.

Project Thirty-six

PERSPECTIVE: MULTIPLE VANISHING POINTS

In Figure 56 in one-point perspective all of the forms projected into perspective are at right angles or are parallel to the picture plane. In Figure 48 we observed a series of cubes from directly in front of the forward corner; consequently, an equal amount of the two visible sides of the cube can be seen. In such an instance there are two vanishing points, one for each of the sets of parallel

Detail from Perspective Study for "Adoration of the Magi,"
Leonardo da Vinci. Drawing, Figure 14–4.
Uffizi Gallery, Florence.

57. *One-point perspective.*

58. *One-point perspective.*
"Figures and Animals in Deep Architectural View,"
Gaetano Gondolfi. Drawing, Figure 14–3.
Los Angeles County Museum.

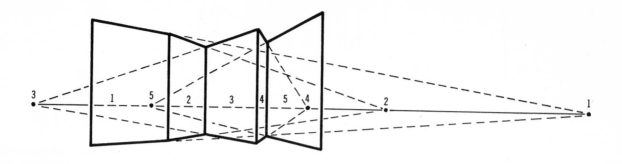

59. A five-faceted screen with five vanishing points. The more closely a plane approximates being at right angles to the picture plane, the more central is the vanishing point. Conversely, the more closely a plane approximates being parallel to the picture plane, the farther from the center is the vanishing point.

lines receding into space, and the two vanishing points are equidistant from the center of the drawing. In Figure 51, cubes 1, 2, and 3 reveal uneven amounts of the two visible sides, indicating that the viewer is not directly in front of the forward corner of the sphere. As a consequence the vanishing points for the two sides are not equidistant from the center of the drawing for the following reason. The more closely a plane in a drawing approximates being at right angles to the picture plane, the closer is its vanishing point to the center of the drawing (remember that when a plane *is* at right angles to the picture plane its vanishing point is in the center of the drawing). The more closely a plane in a drawing approximates being parallel to the picture plane, the farther is its vanishing point from the center of the drawing. This concept is illustrated in Figure 59. This drawing of a five-faceted screen employs five vanishing points, since no two facets of the screen parallel one another. Notice that vanishing point 4, the vanishing point for plane 4, the plane closest to being at right angles to the picture plane, is closest to center. Vanishing point 1, the vanishing point for plane 1, the plane most close to paralleling the picture plane, is the farthest from center. Draw a multifaceted screen and project each facet to its vanishing point.

Project Thirty-seven

PERSPECTIVE: MULTIPLE VANISHING POINTS

Study Figure 60. In this sketch one finds two sets of vanishing points (four vanishing points), one set for the group of skyscrapers in the back plane, another for the low buildings that touch the picture plane in the foreground. All the left-hand planes on the back range of buildings vanish at point A, located on the left-hand border of the drawing. The vanishing point for the right-hand planes of this set of buildings (the facets that are shaded with diagonal lines) would be located far out of the picture at the right. The vanishing points for the left facets and top planes of the front range of buildings is located at point B, almost in the center of the drawing, and the other set of vanishing points for the shaded facets of the front buildings would be even farther to the right than that for the back range of buildings since the front planes come even closer to being parallel to

60. *Two groups of buildings not parallel to one another with two sets of vanishing points (four vanishing points).*

the picture plane. In this drawing, therefore, because there are two sets of rectangular forms pictured, neither parallel or at right angles to one aonther, four vanishing points are used even though only two are apparent in this sketch. Place two large cartons or boxes before you so that the sides are neither parallel to the picture-plane nor to one another and draw them. When you have completed the drawing, project the major planes into perspective to ascertain whether or not your vanishing points have been correctly placed. If you have made mistakes, correct the drawing. Study Figure 61, "View with a Villa and Building at Left," by Dominico Fossati. Here, too, two sets of vanishing points have been used, one for the building at the extreme left which also serves for the tall cypresses and the left facet of the wall which encloses them, the other set which serves for the buildings at the right. You will find that Fossati has permitted himself a certain amount of license in relation to the consistency of horizon line and vanishing points. However, the effect is convincing because the chief perspective systems work in relation to one another.

Project Thirty-eight

PERSPECTIVE: MULTIPLE HORIZON LINES

So far in our discussion it has been implied that all vanishing points are on the horizon line. This is only true of vanishing points for those sets of lines which define planes parallel to the ground plane. All of the forms described in Figures 1 to 8 being rectangular, and

61. *Perspective study with two sets of vanishing points.*
"View with Villa and a Building at Left," Domenico Fossati
(1743–1784; Italian). *Sepia and pen wash, 8½" x 15½".*
Los Angeles County Museum of Art.

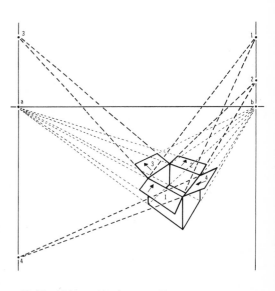

resting flat on the ground plane, converge to vanishing points on the horizon line.

Figure 62 introduces the use of vanishing points which are not located on the horizon line. Of the six vanishing points used in drawing the carton with open flaps, only vanishing points A and B are located on the horizon for they are the vanishing points for those edges of the carton and flaps which are parallel to the ground plane. However, each of the open flaps 1, 2, 3, and 4 moves into space at an angle that is not parallel to the ground plane, so each of these flaps has vanishing points above or below the horizon line. Study the relationship between each open flap and its vanishing point, noting that the more vertical the plane, the higher the vanishing point. We must then amend a previous statement which says that all sets of parallel lines drawn in perspective converge as they recede into space to meet at vanishing points on the horizon line. Instead, let us say that all sets of parallel lines drawn in perspective converge as they recede into space to meet at a vanishing point in the distance. While the exact location of each vanishing point can be determined by scientific perspective this involves more elaborate theories and skills than are necessary for general sketching. (The vanishing points of inclined planes do not fall on the horizon of the ground plane, but on a vertical line drawn through a vanishing point of the horizontal plane. The vanishing point of an ascending plane will be above the horizon, that of a descending plane is below the horizon. The position of the vanishing points on the vertical line is determined by the angle of the plane.) It is more important for our purposes to develop the ability to *observe* the convergences that occur as planes pitched at various angles move in space than to ascertain the exact vanishing points for the various planes. Compare Figure 63 with the previously discussed Figure 62. In Figure 62 the flaps of the carton were drawn in perspective to converge at points 1, 2, 3 and 4. In Figure 63, being drawn contrary to the laws of perspective, the flaps cease to appear as true rectangles but appear to be irregular trapazoids. Beginners frequently draw slanting roofs so they appear wider in back than in front. Compare Figure 64a, where the roof plane converges as it goes into the distance, with Figure 64b, in which the slanting roof is incorrectly drawn.

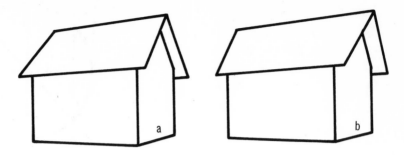

64. A *pitched roof in* (a) *correct and*
(b) *incorrect perspective.*

63. *Carton with vanishing points in incorrect perspective. Convergences and vanishing points are inconsistent.*

Place a large open carton with flaps extended at various angles on the floor and make a free-hand drawing of it in perspective. After you have finished your drawing, project the perspective to vanishing points. Correct any mistakes. Change the angles of the open flaps and draw the carton in another position; profiting by the previous mistakes. Make a drawing of a small house with a pitched roof and gables and place the sides of the roof into perspective. Be certain to observe the roof areas carefully and do not show surfaces you cannot see. It is most important to integrate perspective theory with drawing habits.

Project Thirty-nine

PERSPECTIVE: ELLIPSES

So far our study of perspective has concerned itself with the perspective of rectangular forms. Circles, ovals, and other curvilinear forms need separate consideration. The circle provides the basic curvilinear form for the study of perspective since an understanding of the perspective of circles will help when sketching more complex curves.

When a circle goes into perspective it assumes the form of an ellipse. The exact form of an ellipse can best be understood if the circle is placed in a square and the square is projected into perspective (Figure 65a,b). To place the circle and square meaningfully in perspective it is necessary to first visualize a circle in a square seen not in perspective but full face (Figure 65a). Notice the location of lines a–a, b–b, c–c, and d–d, for these provide guide lines that enable us to foreshorten the circle form accurately. Now study Figure 65b carefully, and you will see that all of the elements in Figure 65a have been placed in perspective in Figure 65b. Observe that the elliptical form created where the edges of the circle touch the sides of the square are not pointed but rounded, and that the front half of the circle in perspective is larger than the back half, producing a fuller curve in front. The most frequent mistakes made in drawing ellipses free hand are to draw the more distant curve larger and to make the corners too pointed as in Figure 66. Project two or

THE ART ELEMENTS

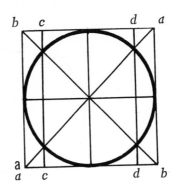

three circular forms placed in squares in varying degrees of perspective and then draw some ellipses free hand.

Project Forty

PERSPECTIVE: ELLIPSES IN VARYING PERSPECTIVES

If a glass cylinder with a circular top and bottom is held in a sequence of positions from far below the eye to high above, one will observe that the circle is seen almost in the full round when it is far below the eye or far above it. As the circle approaches eye level a sequence of increasingly closed ellipses are seen that become a straight line at eye level (Figure 67b). The same phenomenon occurs when a circle is viewed moving from a position far to either side to a position directly in front of the observer (Figure 67a). Place a cylindrical object on the floor in front of you, and then in increasingly high positions until it is at eye level. Draw it in a sequence of such positions. Continue placing the object above your eye level and continue to draw the circular shapes of the top as you look up at them. Draw a wheeled object going into perspective, a bicycle, car, child's wagon, or any other convenient source of circular shapes.

Project Forty-one

PERSPECTIVE: ELLIPSES IN AN ARCHITECTURAL SETTING

A number of problems involving ellipses appear when one is sketching traditional architecture of any complexity. Arches, circular windows, the capitals and bases of columns, round turrets and towers, all involve the perspective of circles and partially circular forms. These circular elements usually appear along with rectangular forms, and if they are not handled consistent with the rectangular forms the drawing will be weakened. Frequently it is wise to use bisected squares (Figures 65a,–b) as a basis for making ellipses, particularly when drawing a series of arches going into perspective, as in a long arcade. Draw architectural subjects that involve arches or other circular forms.

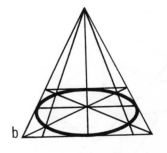

65. (a) *A circle in perspective.* (b) *To project the circle into accurate perspective it has been placed within a square.*

*66. Ellipses
incorrectly drawn.*

■ *Perspective: Sketchbook*

Continuous practice in perspective drawing sensitizes the eye so that one unconsciously sees in perspective and can readily perceive errors. In your sketchbook sketch subjects, both from theory and observation, that involve perspective: books, boxes, furniture, room interiors, buildings, street scenes, automobiles, boats, machine forms, and so on. When you draw objects such as automobiles or boats it is frequently helpful to place them in a theoretical "box" or draw the forms as though they were encased in rectangular blocks and then modify the rectangular into ovoid forms. In drawing complex architectural subjects, particularly outdoor buildings, you will frequently be hard put to tell whether the edges of forms appear to rise or fall as they go into the distance. Even using your pencil as a horizontal plumb line to judge the degree and direction of angle will not always reveal the proper cues. In such cases ask yourself whether the confusing edge is *above* or *below* your eye level. If your eye is 5 feet from the ground and a roof line is 8 feet above the ground *and* the ground on which you are located is approximately level with the ground on which the building is located, the roof edge must *descend* toward the horizon as it goes from you into the distance. With much drawing and much looking uncertainties become less frequent and drawing becomes more accurate. Accuracy in itself is no great virtue in drawing, and mechanical modes of procedure that inhibit freedom and instill habits of undue timidity and caution are more harmful than the faults they are meant to correct. Draw frequently, vigorously and freely, continuously looking *at* the subject of your drawing. After you have drawn an object study the drawing and ask yourself whether your position in space in relation to the object is properly conveyed by the drawing. If not, check on the implied horizon line, the location of your implied vanishing points and make the necessary corrections. The most frequent mistakes are (1) drawing as though you had a bird's-eye view of objects so that the converging perspective lines meet high above the buildings, (2) not having related sets of converging perspective lines meet at common vanishing points, (3) drawing ellipses with pointed corners and having the fuller curve on an ellipse on the farther rather than the closer side.

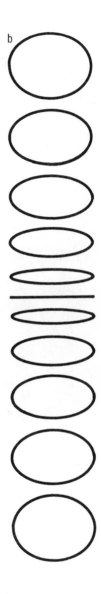

Note that in Figure 61 there tends to be convergence to a general area rather than to exact vanishing points. Early in the Renaissance it was discovered that more than one horizon line was frequently useful in a complex composition in that it produced a more lifelike, multiple-focused effect than adherence to a rigid, single-focused horizon line. It should be mentioned here, also, that many fine drawings violate conventional perspective concepts, but our subject, at the moment, is perspective.

Many aspects of perspective have not been touched on here. Our purpose has been to introduce the subject in a simple way to provide the beginner with sufficient working skills to handle general sketching requirements. There are, however, a number of theoretical and practical books on perspective for the student who wishes further study in this area. One of the best very simple books is *Perspective Made Easy*, by Ernest Norling (New York: The Macmillan Company, 1940).

■ *Values: Pattern*

The introduction to a discussion of pattern on page 326 of *Drawing* reads, "Flat unmodulated surfaces carry as pattern, rather than as form. We see the shape of the area, are conscious of its silhouette, but the sense of volume is minimized." Accompanying an increased consciousness of pattern is an awareness of decorative qualities. When a pattern is used for decorative purposes its chief role is to embellish rather than to represent or symbolize. Most textile patterns have this decorative function; the essential role of the design is to enrich the surface of the cloth irrespective of whether or not it is representational, symbolic or abstract. A silhouette, whether black on white or white on black, provides the greatest possible value simplification. It is not, however, sufficiently complex to be very entertaining. "J'ai Baisé ta Bouche, Jokanaan," by Aubrey Beardsley, *Drawing* (Figure 8–12), or the more simplified final version (Figure 68), reveals far greater complexity than a pure silhouette, with a consequent increase of visual interest. In the lower third of the composition the patterns are white on a black ground, the

67. *Circles in perspective.* (*a*) *The ellipses formed as circles move from far left to far right of the viewer.* (*b*) *Circles moving from far below to far above the eye level of the viewer.*

68. *Black and white pattern.*
Illustration for "Salome,"
Aubrey Beardsley. Also see
Drawing, *Figure 8–12.* Princeton
University Library, Princeton, N.J.

central and upper right areas have black patterns and lines on a white ground, the upper left again reverses the order. Some elements in the drawing, such as the faces of the two principals and Salome's robes, are outlined so that an effect of white pattern on white ground provides a still further enrichment of the decorative scheme. In the upper left corner white lines have been used on a black ground to outline the circle-scale patterns and create an effect of black pattern on black.

Project Forty-two

VALUE: PATTERN, BLACK AND WHITE

Choose a subject and plan a composition or select one of your previous drawings which you feel has decorative pattern potentialities. (One of your still-life studies or a symbolic drawing (Project Ten) might be effective.) Sketch your composition in light outlines, and with soft pencil plan where you will place the black masses, white

THE ART ELEMENTS

69. *Black, white, and gray pattern.*
Detail from "The Doorbell,"
Matt Kahn. Drawing, *Figure*
14–16. Collection of the artist.

masses, and where you will use black outlines on white and leave
white outlines on black. Finish the study using brush and ink. If
you wish a more refined drawing than your present equipment permits, you can purchase kid bristol-board and a metal pen point: The
kid bristol-board provides a brilliant white, takes the ink well, and
permits fine pen lines of even width.

Project Forty-three

VALUE: PATTERN, BLACK, WHITE, AND GRAY

The use of intermediate values of gray provides for an additional
enrichment of a black and white decorative pattern. In a detail from
"The Doorbell" (Figure 69) the soft grays make the blacks and
whites seem even more vivid, sharp and dramatic. The fact that
"The Doorbell" is symbolic and expressive in no way diminishes its
decorative value; in fact, its symbolic character adds to its interest.
For the ensuing problems use a previous drawing or choose a new
subject. You might find it intriguing to translate a sound effect
("telephone," "chimes," or some favorite piece of music) into patterns. Or, since the gray you will use can have a strong textural

character, you might take a material such as velvet, satin, or drift-wood, and develop an abstract-symbolic pattern that expresses in visual terms the textural and physical character of the material. Make a preliminary sketch with pencil or charcoal on newsprint, planning, first, the shapes and then the placement of blacks, whites, and grays. Draw your composition in light pencil. For your grays crush a bit of compressed charcoal and apply it to your paper with a soft cloth or a piece of paper toweling, rubbing it gently into the paper until you have smooth gradations of the desired values. Use India ink for your blacks. If, on completion of the assignment the white areas have lost their brilliance because of smudges, clean them with a soft eraser.

Both "J'ai Baisé ta Bouche, Jokanaan" and "The Doorbell" exploit full contrasts of value with vigor. Value schemes which are limited in their range of dark and light also have their effectiveness, as is indicated in the discussion on pages 327 to 331 of *Drawing*. The discussion on those pages might be summarized as follows: Close value relationships in which contrasts are minimized are used to create effects of quiet, soothing restfulness, or of introspection and restraint. Predominantly dark compositions suggest night, darkness, mystery, and fear. Predominantly light value patterns carry implications of illumination, clarity, and suggest a rational and optimistic attitude toward life.

Project Forty-four

VALUE: CLOSELY RELATED VALUES

Select a theme that seems appropriate for a study in close value relationships such as "Twilight," "Gray Day," or "Contemplation." If you cannot get an idea that suggests a composition in close value relationships, select one of your previous drawings and use it as the basis for the following exercise: Enclose an area the size of this *Study Guide* in charcoal or pencil, depending upon your preference, using either charcoal paper or newsprint. Use crushed charcoal or graphite obtained by rubbing a soft pencil lead on fine sandpaper. Using a piece of cloth or paper towel as an applicator, rub on an

70. *Light values made evident by dark accents. Detail of "Standing Figure," Wayne Thiebaud. Drawing, Figure 12–14. Collection of the artist.*

even tone of medium-light gray over the entire enclosed rectangle. Develop your composition by adding darker lines and tones of gray, and erasing out lighter areas and lines. Avoid intense blacks and pure white lights so that a gray effect prevails.

Project Forty-five

VALUE: DARK VALUES

Select a theme that will lend itself to a predominantly dark composition. Night subjects are, of course, ideal, but a wide variety of either representational or symbolic concepts can be given intensity through the use of extended areas of dark with small amounts of accent in light or middle value gray. Plan your composition for execution in either charcoal or charcoal and ink. If you use only charcoal you may wish to do a full-page composition. If you use ink and charcoal you might better contain your composition within a rectangle the size of the *Study Guide*. If your lights or whites become smudged they can be erased clean when the drawing is completed or can be reinforced with white chalk. Add India-ink blacks over the darkest charcoal areas. If the ink appears to separate visually from the darkest charcoal areas you might use a textured or dry-brush application of ink to provide a transition from ink to charcoal. For dry-brush effects partially fill your brush with India ink and then remove excess ink by drawing the brush over newsprint paper or blotter. When the amount of ink left in the brush is such that a light swipe of the brush against paper leaves a granular texture, proceed to create a transitional texture tone between the solidly inked masses and the darkest charcoal areas.

Project Forty-six

VALUE: LIGHT VALUES

Because we ordinarily draw upon white or light paper one sees more drawings that carry as light value compositions than in other value schemes.

Most drawings done in hard pencil and most drawings done in line, irrespective of medium, carry as essentially light-value drawings. It is only by the extensive application of light grays, or by the strategic use of a few very dark accents, as with Thibaut's "Standing Figure" (Figure 70), that the observer becomes aware of a predominantly pale tone.

As in the two previous projects, select a subject that is well adapted to this particular value range. If such a theme is not forthcoming, select one of your previous drawings and treat it as a composition in light values of gray. You might frame a rectangle the size of the *Study Guide* and then rub in a small amount of graphite until you have an even tone of pale gray. Using a fairly hard pencil (2H or 3H) to delineate your composition, add pencil middle value accents and erase out lights. If you need a few darks for emphasis, use a soft pencil. Hard pencil makes a pale gray line. When used with skill on very white, fine paper, such as the kid Bristol previously recommended for pen and ink, effects of great elegance can be achieved (Figure 71).

THE ART ELEMENTS

71. *Hard pencil and rubbed graphite on Bristol board.*
"Wild Radish," D. Mendelowitz. 15½" x 21½".
Collection of the author.

Project Forty-seven

VALUE: VALUE CONTRASTS FOR EMPHASIS

Contrasts of value provide one of the most effective means for accenting and emphasizing areas in a composition. Variations in degrees of dark and light, along with the linear elements, create focal points which can direct the viewer's attention to parts of the composition according to their degree of importance. Focusing attention through contrast of value works equally well whether a composition is representational or abstract, as can be observed by comparing Sir

72. *Texture study.*
Enlarged drawing of 1″ x 1¼″ section
of natural sponge. Pencil 4″ x 5″.

David Wilkie's "Arrival of the Rich Relation" with Calvin Albert's "Ritual" or Hans Hartung's "D. 42.2" (*Drawing*, Figures 17–6, 10–8, 1–19).

Draw a rectangle around the *Study Guide* and divide the area into rectangles of sufficiently varying sizes to make an interesting composition with three areas designed to serve as points of focus. In each case the point of focus might be a small rectangle composed within the larger ones. Using compressed charcoal to create different grays, place varying values of gray, black, and white in the rectangular areas so that the boldest contrasts will occur where you have planned your focal points. Your strongest contrasts would logically be created by small black rectangles on a white ground, or vice versa. Compose a second abstract composition using a variety of shapes, geometric, biomorphic or organic, and plan one major center of interest and two minor ones. Again plan the contrasts of value to focus attention on parts of the composition according to their importance. Draw a composition of a still life or any other subject you prefer or take any previous assignment that you think will provide a good subject and plan a composition with representational forms which will have a clearly established center of interest and minor centers of interest. Execute in dark and light in soft pencil or charcoal.

■ *Texture*

Read Chapter 15, in *Drawing*, on Texture. When we look at the world about us we are not only conscious of form, space, color, and dark and light but we are also continuously aware of tactile qualities, a sense of the feel of surfaces, of roughness and smoothness or hardness and softness. We also unconsciously sense that what we see as a surface is frequently made up of a multitude of small parts. These awarenesses are conveyed by the term *texture*. "Three factors determine the textural character of a drawing. First, in those works concerned with picturing objects there is the surface quality of the objects represented. Second, there are the textures inherent in the artist's materials: coarse chalk on rough paper as contrasted to fine pencil on smooth paper. Third, there is the suggestion of roughness or smoothness that results from the artist's manner of work." These elements, the surface portrayed, the medium and ground, and the method of application, combine to create the textural character of a drawing. Drawings that do not convey a decisive sense of texture, like drawings that do not have an interesting linear quality or characterful value patterns tend to appear flaccid and weak.

Project Forty-eight

TEXTURE: REPRESENTING TEXTURE

Most textures result from the structure and minute moldings of a surface, many of which are so fine that the surface character is difficult to perceive. Also, many surfaces are so familiar that we tend to take them for granted and are not analytical as to their textural character. Enlarging the scale of a surface provides an excellent means of becoming aware of its exact character (Figure 72). The texture of many a familiar surface, for instance, a sponge, a leaf with unusual veining, or the skin of a cantaloupe, proves fascinating on close examination. Select such a textured surface. Light the surface sharply from above and to one side as this will emphasize texture. Draw a rectangle the size of the *Study Guide* and in pencil fill the rectangle with a drawing of the surface magnified many times. Model the surface in dark and light value to create a maximum sense of its textural character.

Project Forty-nine

TEXTURE: THE TEXTURE OF THE ARTIST'S MATERIALS

For this project you will need to acquire a much greater variety of materials than you have worked with heretofore. Gather pieces of paper with varying degrees of roughness or smoothness and various surface grainings. (These need not be full sheets; pieces with a surface area of only 9 or 10 square inches will suffice.) Gather together as many kinds of chalks, crayons, and pencils as you can find. Collect various types of felt, nylon, and ball-point pens, as well as brushes that can be used for applying ink. Proceed to experiment with ways of applying the various media you have collected on the different papers. For textural variety try using both the sides and points of dry media, using both cross-hatching and stippling with dry and wet media, and ink applied with various types of pens and brushes. Try combining the various techniques and media. Cut out even-sized areas of the textures which you consider most interesting and mount them on heavy paper or mat board in such a way that differences of texture are emphasized.

Project Fifty

TEXTURE: COMPARATIVE RENDERINGS

Set up a simple still-life subject which has little textural interest, smooth vegetable or fruit forms and a bowl on a table, or a plaster cast. Select two contrasting combinations of media and paper from the previous experiment and render the subject in each combination. Study the two drawings when they are completed and try to determine which method of working seems most satisfying to you, both in terms of enjoying the activity and achieving an effective drawing. Developing a sense of your artistic identity should be both a conscious and an unconscious part of your development as a draftsman.

Project Fifty-one

TEXTURE: EXPLORING PREFERENCES

The freedom or caution with which a medium is applied to paper, the degree to which hands and body are relaxed, all expressions of inner tension or harmony, as well as intellectual convictions and esthetic tastes, work together to form an artist's mature style. Each artist's style has its textural character. The beginner frequently has conscious preferences which take the form of admiration for some particular master's way of working, and very frequently the beginner gives legitimate expression to these preferences by following the manner of the master. Very gradually, as the young artist finds himself, his way of working gains assurance and independence from previously admired models and his own particular style evolves. Study the reproductions in *Drawing*, particularly those in Chapter 15, and select ways of working, the textural character of which appeal to you. Using the media which you feel you handle most effectively, draw simple objects in ways derived from the admired manner. It is important to use similar if not identical materials. Do not try to copy the admired techniques but instead try to feel the mood of the style and the manner in which it was carried out, whether slowly and methodically or rapidly and impulsively, whether with small finger strokes or large hand movements, and so on. After you have made a number of drawings study them in relation to the master drawings that inspired them. Try to discern where your methods and results deviate from your model and to what degree you prefer your deviations. When you find a way of working which appeals to you, either because you feel comfortable when using it or because you like the results, use it in your sketchbook and elsewhere. It is important to discover the ways of working which are most satisfying to you and which you can use with the minimum of self-consciousness.

73a. *Textural interpretation of foliage.*
Detail from "Landscape," Adam
Pynacker. Drawing, *Figure 5–16.*
Allen Memorial Art Museum, Oberlin,
Ohio (F. F. Prentice Fund).

Project Fifty-two

TEXTURE: RENDERING MULTIPLE UNITS AS TEXTURE

In *Drawing*, we read, "Modern students of the psychology of perception have observed that we see similar things as making up a unit. Thus when we look at a tree, we are not aware of the hundreds of leaves that make up the tree, but rather fuse them into a single visual entity . . . a cluster of leaves becomes a tree. When we look at a tree we see its multiple-united surface as a texture, and in rendering the surface an artist tends to suggest that textural character by wiggling the hand, stippling, making lines, splotches, or using any other measures that appropriately suggest the surface quality of the object. Such movements of the hand become almost automatic in time, the hand responding to the visual perception of texture as unconsciously as it responds to changes of direction when one is doing contour drawing. Figure 73 a, b, c, d, e, f, g, h, has details from eight different drawings of foliage by eight artists. The eight artists were representing various trees and using different media; they had been trained in differing traditions, were of divergent temperaments. Study them, analyzing the various ways of suggesting

foliage. Select two or three trees from nature with sharp differences in the character of their foliage. Before you start to draw analyze the elements that give each tree its particular character—the shapes of the foliage masses, the sizes of leaves, whether they hang, radiate from a central point or lie in horizontal or vertical stratas, the size and shape of the areas of sky seen through the masses of foliage, the character of branch patterns where branch pattern is seen, and related factors. After you have analyzed these surface qualities develop textures that communicate the character of the foliage masses, using the medium of your choice. Select the texture that you think most satisfactory and draw a full tree.

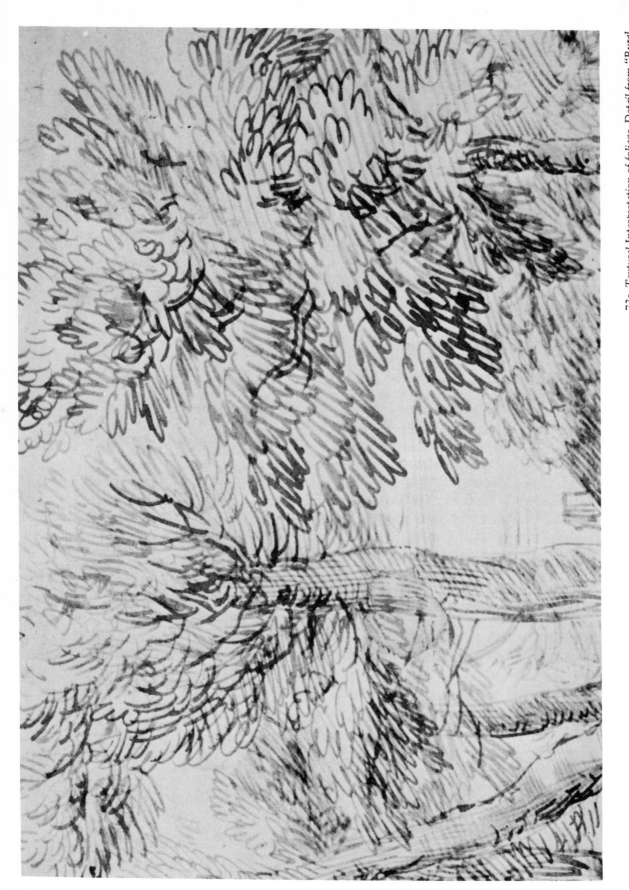

73c. *Textural Interpretation of foliage. Detail from "Rural Landscape with Milkmaid," Jan Lievens. Drawing, Figure 6–5. Metropolitan Museum of Art, New York (Rogers Fund, 1961).*

73d. *Textural interpretation of foliage. Detail from "Weinberg, Olivano, Heinrich Reinhold. Drawing, Figure 7–6. Staatliche Graphische Sammlung, Munich.*

73e. *Textural interpretation of foliage. Detail from "In San Rémy," Vincent Van Gogh. Drawing, Figure 8–9.* Collection of Mrs. Ruth Lilienthal.

73f. *Textural interpretation of foliage. Detail from "Bank of a Pond," Rodolphe Bresdin. Drawing, Figure 15–10.* Art Institute of Chicago (Gift of the Print and Drawing Club).

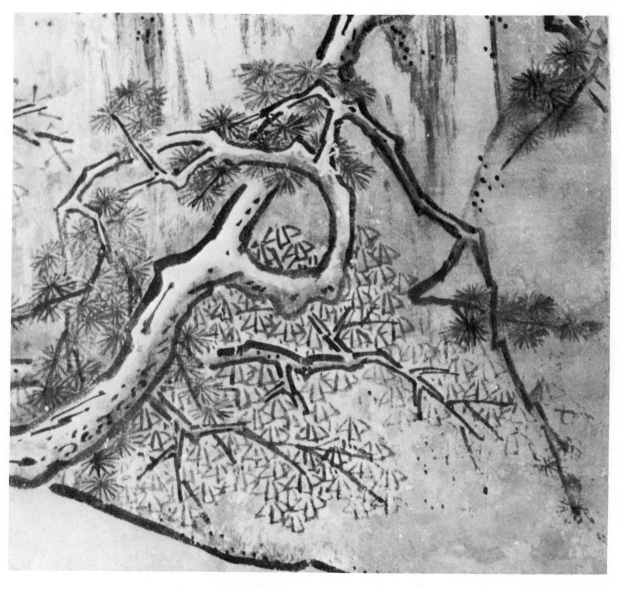

73g. *Textural interpretation of foliage. Detail from
"Panel of a Six-Fold Screen," School of Sesshu.* Drawing,
Figure 17–9. Stanford Museum (Ikeda Collection).

73h. Textural interpretation of foliage.
Detail from "Trees," Harry A. Davis. Drawing, Figure 17–17.
Collection of Mrs. William P. Dawn.

THE ART ELEMENTS

Project Fifty-three

TEXTURE: STUDIED AND FREE RENDERING

Look about you and make a list of interesting textures: grass, various tree barks, gravel, hair, shingle, shake, tile, field stone, cut stone, brick, velvet, satin, corduroy, and so forth. Using the various media which seem logical for the surfaces, analyze and deliberately reproduce a small area of each surface. Then proceed to suggest various surfaces by less deliberate and more spontaneous renderings. Select a subject in which there is ample opportunity to convey a vivid variety of textures (a landscape often provides such subject matter). Using a medium which seems well suited to the subject, proceed to draw it so as to create a drawing of as vivid a textural character as possible. Remember that the textural character of a drawing is created by an interplay between the subject, the medium and the artist's personality. Remember that vivid textural character is not synonymous with a bold manner, as can be seen by again studying the various renderings of trees.

Project Fifty-four

TEXTURE: THE UNIFORM TEXTURE

Some artists prefer to draw in such a way that the textural character of a drawing assumes an abstract character, not determined by the subject being portrayed, but rather by the mode of applying the medium. In such cases a uniform texture is frequently maintained throughout a drawing. This method tends to give a certain formality to a drawing and seems best suited to stylized modes of expression, as can be seen in details from Van Rysellberghe's "Maria van de Velde at the Piano," Léger's "The Divers," Seurat's "Sous la Lampe," Gleizes' "Port" (Figure 74a, b, c, and 39). These uniform textures almost have the character of a texture pattern, since uniformity emphasizes the patternlike aspects of texture.

Enclose five rectangles, roughly 2 inches wide by 3 inches high and fill them with textures of uniform character created in ways sug-

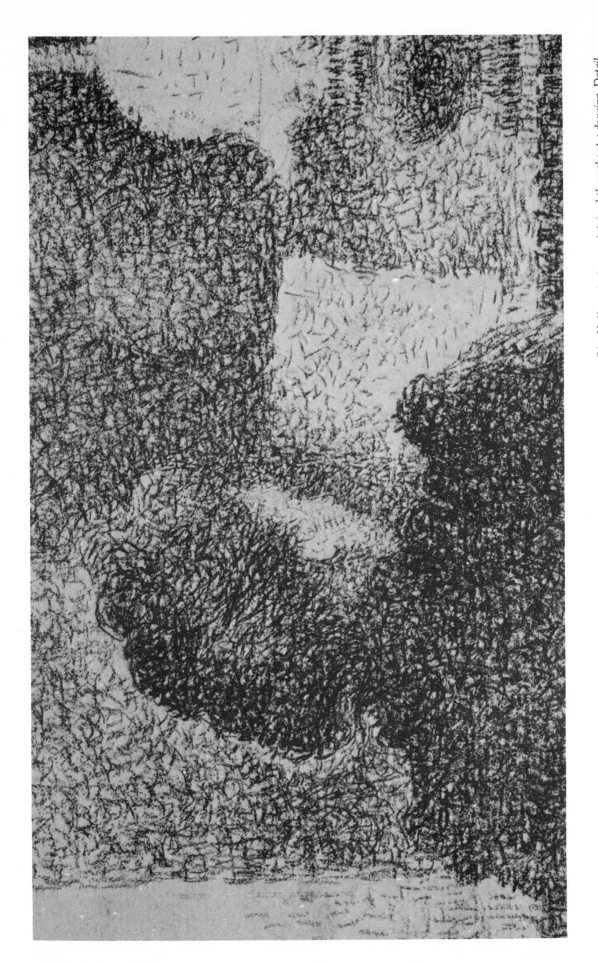

74a. *Uniform texture maintained throughout a drawing. Detail of "Maria van der Welde at the Piano," Théophile Rysselberghe. Drawing, Figure 15–9. Art Institute of Chicago (John H. Wrenn Fund).*

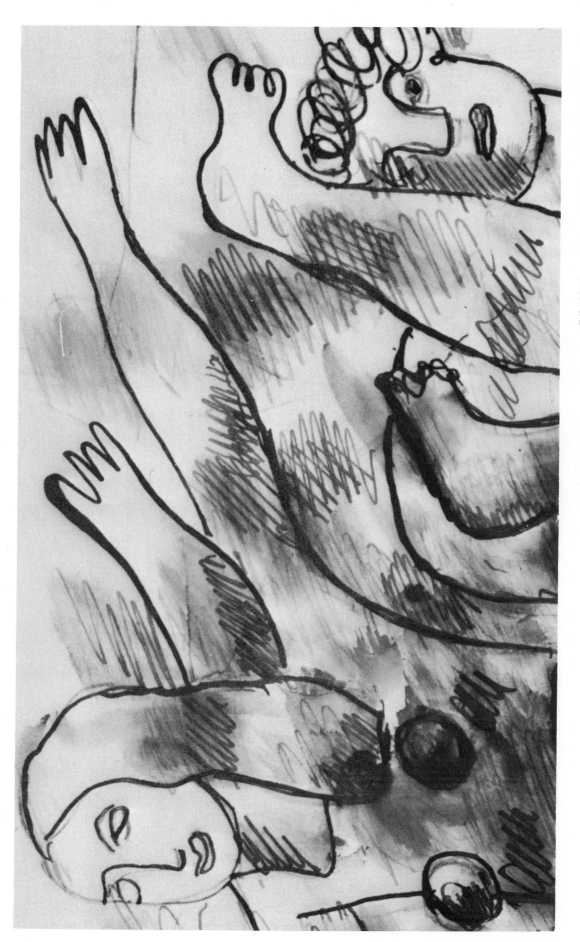

74b. *Uniform texture. Detail from "Study for "The Divers,"" Fernand Léger. Drawing, Figure 15–16. Art Institute of Chicago (Gift of Tiffany and Margaret Blake).*

74c. Uniform texture.
"Sous la Lampe," Georges Seurat.
Charcoal, 9¼" x 12".
Allen Memorial Art Museum,
Oberlin, Ohio (R. T. Miller, Jr. Fund).

gested by the three drawings in Figure 74, or by methods of your own devising. Work for an even texture which graduates imperceptibly from very dark in one corner to very light in the opposite corner. To create a texture of uniform character, pencil, hard chalk, or ink used with either brush or pen, or both, is preferable to charcoal, since charcoal, being soft, is apt to blur as you work over it. Your gradations of value can be achieved by both darkness of mark and spacing the elements further apart. Some suggested ways of working are: (1) scribble, using curved and circular movements; (2) scribble, using angular and straight-line movements; (3) use straight lines at right angles to one another to create cross-hatched texture; (4) use dots, either being careful to eliminate all linear trailings or consciously use commalike marks; (5) use a combination or modification of one or more of the above suggestions.

THE ART ELEMENTS

Project Fifty-five

TEXTURE: DRAWING DONE WITH A UNIFORM TEXTURE

Select an appropriate subject for drawing or plan a simple composition to be developed in dark and light, using one of the textures devised in Project Fifty-four. If you have difficulty in deciding upon a subject, it might be interesting to use one of your value studies (Projects Forty-two, Forty-three, Forty-four, Forty-five or Forty-six) as the basis for this problem. The size of your drawing should be influenced by the scale of your texture. A coarse brush or soft pencil texture inevitably demands a much larger composition than a fine, precisely applied pen-and-ink or hard-pencil texture.

part 3

DRAWING MEDIA

B Y NOW you have become acquainted with the media most commonly used by beginning students in drawing—pencil, charcoal, brush and ink, and perhaps pen and ink. Chapters 16 and 17 in *Drawing* are designed to further familiarize students with the drawing media most preferred by fine artists of the past. Though there is much experimentation today and many new materials and tools, many fine artists still prefer the traditional media, as can be seen by studying the works of contemporary artists. In Chapter 16, The Dry Media, stick charcoal, compressed charcoal, silverpoint, graphite pencil, chalk, pastel, conté crayon, and scratchboard, are discussed and works executed in the media are reproduced and analyzed. Chapter 17 on The Wet Media presents pen and ink, brush and ink, wash drawing, mixed media, as well as some of the recently developed drawing materials. Exploring a variety of media is important for art students because it enables them to find the medium most precisely suited to their particular tastes and capacities. On the other hand, playing with different media and experimenting with new materials and novel ways of using them can become a pastime and distract students from achieving artistic maturity.

In the following projects, designed to encourage students to explore a wider range of drawing media, there has purposely been an avoidance of what the author considers esoteric and anachronistic media methods and recipes. There is a large body of fascinating literature on the recipes used by the masters of the past for coating paper, making plume and reed pens, iron gall ink, chalks, pastels, brushes and other tools and materials. Many of these recipes render very beautiful and unique results, and they can be rewarding for the occasional mature artist who cannot get the effects he desires from available media. But the time spent on such activities cannot be justified for the young student, who should devote his full time and energies to the major problems of artistic development and self-discovery.

The author has also tried to avoid unduly detailed directives as to the use of media, tools, and materials. Restrictive directions as to how to hold tools and step-by-step instructions for working can make for self-conscious and mechanical procedures, inhibiting rather than furthering the direct and vigorous expression of native capacities. No two individuals are temperamentally alike, and, in general, after accepting certain fundamental and very general procedures, artists work out their own methods. One should play freely with media before embarking upon their use, for only by a free and inventive manipulation of materials do artists discover and develop their personal preferences and ways of working. It is suggested that individuals read through this entire section and then select those media and exercises that sound interesting.

■ *Charcoal*

In the Introduction a few simple exercises were suggested to acquaint beginners with the use of charcoal. Since then it has been suggested that charcoal be used for a number of different drawing problems.

75. *Fully developed charcoal study*
using both the point and side of the charcoal.
Detail of "Self-Portrait," Gustave Courbet. Drawing, Figure 7–13.
Wadsworth Atheneum, Hartford.

You probably realize by now that either stick or compressed charcoal is well adapted to three methods of work: (1) quick sketching; (2) making large-scale studies and preliminary compositional plans that demand a rapidly applied and readily erased medium with which value relationships can be easily visualized; (3) making fully developed, large-scale, dark and light studies. Such studies may be executed with a direct free attack, using both the point and the side of the charcoal for the darks (Figure 75). An alternate method, frequently sought after by enthusiasts for a disciplined rather "pure" use of charcoal, is to build value relationships through systematically cross-hatched lines applied with a pointed stick of charcoal (Figure 76). A clearly grained texture without any of the soft fluidity of tone that accompanies rubbing is considered most desirable in this technique. A third method of applying charcoal produces carefully developed value studies through repeated applications of charcoal carefully rubbed into the paper with either the fingers or a charcoal paper stump (Figure 41).

Project Fifty-six

MEDIA: CHARCOAL: QUICK SKETCHING

Sketch a life model (nude or clothed) in one-minute, five-minute and ten-minute poses. Use a short piece of stick or compressed charcoal (an inch or an inch-and-a-half length usually works well). Keep the flat side of the charcoal against the paper, and use a back and forth motion to rapidly build broad areas of dark. As you sketch, pay as much attention to the shapes of the dark and light areas as you do to contours.

Quick sketching of the kind that is ordinarily done in the life class is valuable in that it develops the capacity to rapidly put down the essential elements of a pose without becoming distracted by the minor details, thus learning to identify the characterizing aspects of a personality type, a gesture or a position. Forcing oneself to make the same kinds of rapid summaries of the characterizing aspects of buildings, trees, vehicles, animals, figures seen on the street, and so on is equally important. Make a group of drawings of such subjects

76. *Fully developed charcoal study*
using only the point of the charcoal.
Detail of "I Know Not Why," R. Baxter. Drawing, Figure 16–4.
Collection of the artist.

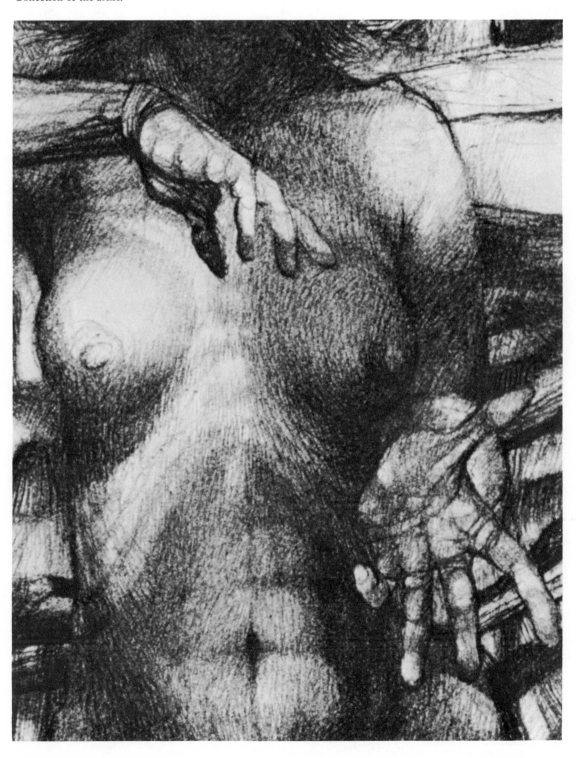

77. *Charcoal applied with both the side and point*
of stick combined with rubbed effects.
Detail of "Ritual," Calvin Albert.
Drawing, *Figure 10–8.*
Art Institute of Chicago.

in charcoal, trying to get the essential character of a form down in one minute, five minutes and ten minutes.

Project Fifty-seven

MEDIA: CHARCOAL: FINISHED COMPOSITION

Before embarking upon a highly finished charcoal drawing it is wise to establish a preliminary visualization of the full linear and tonal compositional arrangement as rapidly as possible. Select your subject. A complex still life or abstraction, a landscape, a cityscape, or a self-portrait are good subjects, provided they encompass a wide range of value relationships. Plan your composition on a piece of newsprint—drawing and redrawing until the arrangement satisfies you. Using the side of a short piece of charcoal, lay in the darks. When you have determined the full value pattern for your composition, pin your preliminary study on the wall where you can see it and using charcoal paper, proceed with your finished drawing. Three methods for making fully developed, large-scale, dark and light charcoal studies are described and illustrated on page 102, Figures 75, 76, 41. Finish your drawing in any one of the three methods according to your preference. It is possible to combine these methods to create further variations of texture, but in so doing, care must be taken to achieve consistency of handling throughout the drawing (Figure 77).

■ *Chalk*

Chalks differ in texture from hard to soft and crumbly to smooth, depending upon the binder used in making them. Many of the chalks commonly used in drawing resemble compressed charcoal; in fact, compressed charcoal might be considered a black chalk made from carbon. The chief advantage that chalks have over compressed charcoal is that chalks come in a range of colors, and this provides both for charming decorative effects and by using dark and light chalks on a middle value paper makes possible the rapid visualization of tonal relationships (Figure 78a, b).

78a. *Light and dark chalk on toned paper. Detail of "Four Studies of Italian Actors," Jean Antoine Watteau. Drawing, Figure 6–10 (see also Plate 10).* Art Institute of Chicago (Gift of Tiffany and Margaret Blake).

78b. *Light and dark chalk on toned paper. Detail of "La Source,"*
Pierre Paul Prud'hon. Drawing, *Figure 7–2 (see also Plate 12).*
Sterling and Francine Clark Art Institute, Williamstown, Mass.

Project Fifty-eight

CHALK: LIGHT AND DARK ON TONED PAPER

Select a subject that will encourage a full range of darks and lights. The subjects suggested for Project Fifty-seven would also work well here. Select a toned charcoal paper of middle value. Execute your composition in dark chalk and a very light chalk, allowing the paper to carry as a middle value. To the degree that you can, avoid smearing the dark and light chalk together as the paper should provide the fusing element. Create your value sequence by adding darks where you want to go darker than the paper value, and light when you want lighter values than the background. If you do not have chalks, this exercise can be done with compressed charcoal and white blackboard chalk.

If you have done Project Fifty-seven in black and white on gray paper, you might enjoy doing another using colored paper and colored chalks. Select a dark tan paper for use with cream and dark brown chalks, a blue-gray, for use with pale and very dark blue chalks, and so on. The best effect is achieved when the papers and chalks are very closely related in color, without strong differences in intensity, and equidistant in values.

■ *Pastels*

Pastels are varieties of soft chalk that are manufactured in a wide range of colors. Soft pastels, more traditionally called French pastels, come in round sticks, and tend to be very soft and crumbly. They are well adapted to the exercise suggested above. Hard pastels, a more recent development, come in rectangular sticks and bright colors and are made with a semigreasy binder to produce, as the name suggests, a firm-textured chalk. Hard pastels are by shape and texture well adapted to the project suggested below for conté crayon.

Project Fifty-nine

CONTÉ CRAYON

Conté crayon is a semihard chalk of fine texture with a sufficiently oily binder so that it adheres readily to smooth paper and does not dust off easily. Conté is manufactured in sticks about one-fourth inch square and 3 inches long in varying degrees of hardness. It is usually available in black, white, dark brown, and Venetian red. Drawings done in Venetian red conté are often called sanguine drawings. Conté is usually used in sketching so as to take advantage of the rectangular format, the flat side being used against the paper to create broad strokes of graduated tones, while the corners make elegant, sharply accented lines (Figure 79). Conté is not easily erased and consequently best serves the needs of fairly experienced draftsmen who do not find it necessary to make many changes or corrections when drawing.

Break a stick of conté in two or three pieces and do fairly rapid drawings of posed figures, buildings, trees, vehicles, animals, or any other subject that appeals to you. Work for a broad suggestion of essential forms and movements. Build your darker values by using the side of the crayon rather than by cross-hatching lines. The lines created by using the corners of the square provide energetic contrasts.

Project Sixty

CONTÉ CRAYON: FULLY DEVELOPED DRAWING

The fine texture of conté is well adapted to the creation of carefully finished, large drawings with a full value range (Figure 80). If you wish to make such a highly finished drawing in conté select a smooth, firm paper. Decide on your subject and plan your arrangement on newsprint paper until you are fairly certain of your composition. Lay in your initial lines lightly and then proceed to develop your drawing in full value. Drawings done in brown or red conté can often

79. *Twenty-minute life drawing sketch in conté crayon.*
The broad areas of dark were built up with the side of
the crayon, the sharp corners were used for the linear accents.

DRAWING MEDIA

be strengthened with black accents. Drawings done with black, brown, or red conté on gray or tan paper can be effectively highlighted with white conté.

◼ Wax Crayons

There are a number of hard, greasy chalks and wax crayons available to those who want a medium which readily produces strong darks which do not rub or smear. Wax crayons and lithographic crayons have this virtue, but they have the corresponding disadvantage that they do not erase nor can lines or tones be easily fused or blurred. When used on grained papers, vigorous, clearly defined textures can be produced. Students wishing to experiment with any of the hard of greasy wax crayons can follow the general suggestions made for quick sketching with conté. Wax crayons can also be used in a manner similar to charcoal or black chalk.

Charcoal, conté, lithographic crayon and wax crayon all come in pencil form. The pencil form tends to limit the freedom with which they can be used, so that for practical purposes they bear a strong

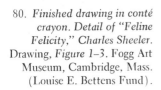

80. *Finished drawing in conté crayon. Detail of "Feline Felicity," Charles Sheeler.* Drawing, *Figure 1–3*. Fogg Art Museum, Cambridge, Mass. (Louise E. Bettens Fund).

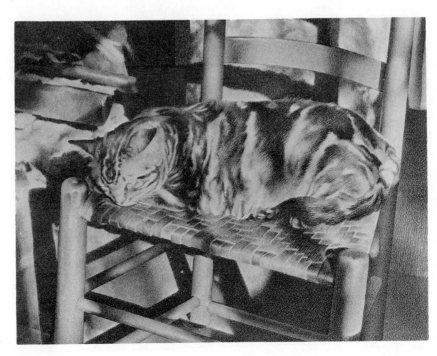

similarity to a soft graphite pencil. Their greatest virtue is that they readily produce more vigorous darks and lack the shine that sometimes is disturbing in drawings done with graphite pencils.

■ *Pencil*

The graphite pencil is familiar to every art student, but because it is familiar its limitations are often not recognized. Pencil is most frequently forced beyond its limit of effectiveness by attempting to build extended areas of dark shading with a hard lead. Soft pencil is sometimes used in broad dark lines for free sketchy effects when chalk, crayon, or charcoal would have been more successful. In general, when an area is overworked in pencil, a shiny, mottled surface ensues, sometimes marked with indentations from repeated pressures of the pencil. When used with limited areas of dark value, pencil operates very handsomely (Figures 71, 81, 82).

Project Sixty-one

PENCIL: THE MODELED LINE

Pencil is particularly well adapted to a type of drawing in which light shading is used in conjunction with line to convey a fuller sense of form than can be suggested by outline alone (Figure 81). Using a fairly hard paper and, according to preference, a pencil somewhere between 3B and H, draw a subject with fairly complex forms and interlacing parts. An arrangement of leaves and flowers, a still-life study with fruits and vegetables, a cast or figure study with the light coming from in front so that there are not extensive, dark shadows provide good subjects for this exercise. Avoid trying to extend the darks over too wide an area or forcing the pencil toward darker values than it produces easily.

Project Sixty-two

PENCIL: SMALL MODELED DRAWINGS

Very small, precise drawings of great elegance can be made by using fairly hard pencils on smooth Bristol board. Select an interesting

81. *Light pencil shading reinforcing pencil outlines.*
Detail of "Study for the Golden Age, "
Jean-Auguste Dominique Ingres. Drawing, *Figure 7–1.*
Fogg Art Museum, Cambridge, Mass.
(Grenville L. Winthrop Collection).

small object, preferably light-colored (Figure 82). Using two pencils, a fairly hard pencil (perhaps a 2H, and a medium, perhaps HB), sketch the object in lightly with the softer pencil and proceed to model it with the harder pencil. Use the softer pencil for the darkest accents. If drawings of this type are too large or the pencil is forced toward darker values than comes easily, the drawings become labored in effect and lose their beauty.

82. *Small drawing done with full shading in hard pencil. "Yellow Rose,"* D. Mendelowitz. 5½" x 7". Collection of the author.

83a. *Pencil suggestions of patterns and textures. Detail of "Old Saw Mill," Louis Michel Eilshemius.* Drawing, *Figure 16–11.* Amherst College, Amherst, Mass.

Project Sixty-three

PENCIL: FORMALIZED PATTERNS

A medium soft pencil, 2B or 3B, is very effective used freely in open, rather formalized linear patterns to provide dark and light interest and suggest texture (Figure 83 a, b). By increasing the scale of cross-hatchings, diagonal line shading and texture-patterns, both descriptive and decorative values are emphasized. Make some sketches of landscape, cityscapes, still life or the costumed figure that will encourage the development of a variety of lively pencil patterns. Do not attempt too much detail, fine-scale patterns, nor extended areas of dark.

84. *Freely scribbled lines reinforced by darker pencil accents.*
"*Interior of the Artist's Studio,*" *Jean Edouard Vuillard (1868–1940; French).*
Pencil, 4½" x 7". Feigen-Palmer Gallery, Chicago.

Project Sixty-four

PENCIL: MEANDERING SCRIBBLED LINES

Soft pencils are well adapted to a free, very open style of sketching. In Figure 84 a meandering line which moves unpredictably in all directions has been used to establish the main forms. Into the matrix of middle dark, sketchy lines, more precise dark lines have been used to define the forms sufficiently to avoid undue ambiguity. Using a 4B and a 6B pencil in a rectangle not to exceed 6 by 10 inches, sketch a landscape, room interior, still life or figure study starting with free, scribbly line movements done with a 4B pencil, later defining the forms more precisely using the 6B pencil for darker accenting lines.

Project Sixty-five

SILVERPOINT

As is pointed out in *Drawing*, metal points are the precursors of pencil. Over the ages silver has seemed to provide the most satisfactory metal point, its lovely gray color oxidizing to a gray-brown with the passing of time. A stout silver wire, not more than one inch long, which can be procured at any jewelry or craft supply house, pointed by rubbing it on sandpaper, provides a satisfactory silverpoint. For ease of handling, the wire can be inserted into a mechanical pencil, a wooden stylus, or a regular wooden pencil from which the lead has been extracted. Any smooth, heavy paper (Bristol board is excellent) surfaced with white poster paint or tempera makes an adequate ground. Silverpoint produces a gray line of even width similar to a hard pencil, and like hard pencil is adapted to making relatively small drawings of exquisite finish. Since lines executed in silverpoint will not blur, gradations of value must be built up through systematic use of diagonal shading, clusters of lines, or cross-hatching (Figure 85). Decide on your subject and proceed as though you were using hard pencil. If you wish to make a pre-

85. *Silverpoint drawing.*
Detail of "Portrait of Frederick
Ashton," Pavel Tchelitchew.
Drawing, *Figure 16–7*. Fogg Art Museum,
Cambridge, Mass.

liminary practice study, you can do so in hard pencil (about 4H). Silverpoint, like scratchboard which is discussed next, is most rewarding to individuals with the craftsman's temperament who enjoy methodical procedures and painstaking workmanship.

86. *Scratchboard techniques.*
(a) Tempera paint coated with
wax crayon. (b) Tempera paint
drawn on with grease pencil.

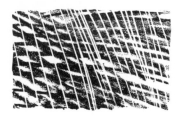

Project Sixty-six

SCRATCHBOARD

Scratchboard is an interesting medium because it reverses the familiar dark on light relationship common to most drawing experiences since the draftsman works with white lines upon a black ground. Like silver point, because the lines will not blur, scratchboard is best adapted to small drawings executed with precision in an essentially linear technique. To produce the ground, heavy poster board should be smoothly coated with white gesso. When dry, this is surfaced with a smooth coat of India ink or fine black tempera. The drawing is then made with a pointed instrument, scratching through the black surface to reveal the white undercoating. Any convenient sharp-pointed metal instrument can be used, such as an etching needle, dentist's tool, or biology dissection instrument.

An easy substitute scratchboard can be made by coating a smooth white hard-surfaced paper with white poster paint and then black

wax crayon. A pointed tool, scalpel or pen-knife blade can then be used to scratch through the layer of black crayon and reveal the white paper underneath (Figure 86). This technique can also be used to make preliminary studies for a project to be executed in scratchboard. Scratchboard provides an excellent medium for planning designs for wood or metal engravings since engraving is also a white-line-on-black-ground technique. Scratchboard works best if there are not extended areas of white to be uncovered, in other words, scratchboard drawings should be essentially white lines on black ground. You might enjoy taking one of your simple line drawings which you like and doing it in scratchboard technique.

An interesting deviation from the full scratchboard drawing technique described above is provided by Monet's "Two Men Fishing" (Figure 87). Monet has drawn upon the white-surfaced paper with grease crayon and then used a sharp instrument to scratch through the crayon lines to reveal clean white accents. If you are interested in attempting a drawing in this technique, coat a piece of white paper with gesso or thick white tempera paint. Draw on the white ground with black wax crayon, lithographic crayon or grease pencil, then with a sharp instrument sketch white lines through the black (Figure 86). This technique is best adapted to a free and sketchy mode of work. You might try it on a small landscape subject.

■ *Pen and Ink*

Pen and ink is unexcelled for certain drawing purposes, although handling it entails a number of difficulties. First of all, unless a superior quality fountain pen is used, the pen, bottle, and dropper are awkward and entail risks, for it is very easy to upset bottles, drip ink onto clothes and furniture, and work. Certainly, pen and ink is ideal for the sketchbook because it does not rub or erase, but carrying the pen and bottle is inconvenient and superior quality fountain pens are expensive and far from trouble-free. For general sketching purposes a pen holder and metal point suffice. A medium-weight point should be used for it produces a vigorous line, neither too thin nor too heavy. Pen points come in a wide range of thicknesses and shapes, and the individual must discover for himself the point that best serves his needs. The cheap ballpoint pens, nylon or felt-tip pens now on the market provide a convenient substitute for traditional pen and ink, although none of them dispense a fluid with the rich opaque dark of India ink, nor do the ball and felt-pen tips have the flexibility of a metal-tip pen. However, the bold lines they produce have their own special character (Figure 88). For use with pen and ink, paper must be smooth and hard: the various Bristol boards, both smooth and kid finish, are ideal. Pen and ink is essentially a linear medium; dark values must be built up line by line and dot by dot. So unless an artist has great technical proficiency, pen and ink should not be used for studies where there are extended areas of dark or subtle gradations from dark to light. Also, pen and ink should not be used for large drawings. None of the following assignments should be larger than this book.

Project Sixty-seven

PEN AND INK: SIMPLE LINE DRAWINGS

The profile drawing of Jean Desbordes by Cocteau, Figure 89, represents the simplest type of pen and ink drawing. The contour line has been put down in discontinuous movements which reflect the artist's sequential observations. Where a mistaken judgment has been corrected, as at the back of the head and neck, the correct line has been

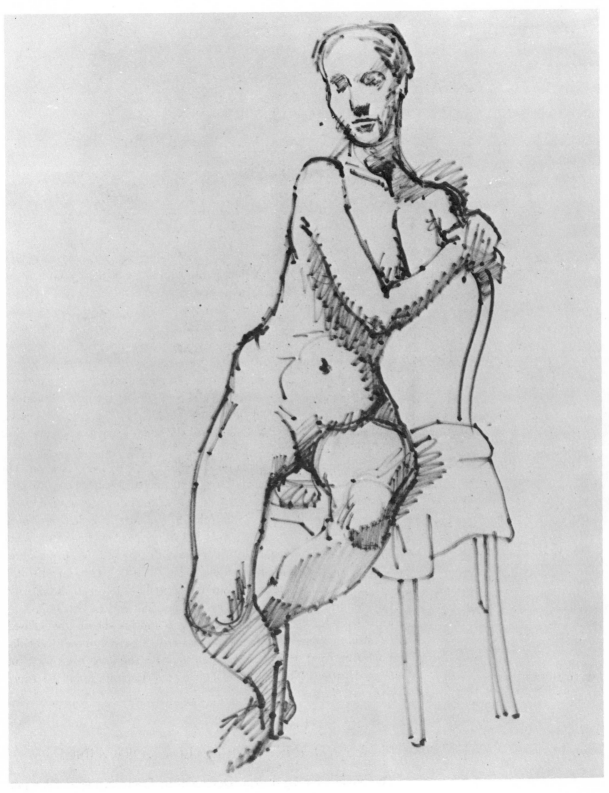

*88. Twenty-minute life drawing
done with felt-tip pen. 18" x 24".*

89. *Pen and ink line drawing.*
"Jean Desbordes," Jean Cocteau. Drawing, *Figure 17–3.*
Art Institute of Chicago (Gift of Mrs. Gilbert W. Chapman
in memory of Charles B. Goodspeed).

90. *Free sketch in pen and ink.*
Detail of "The Sultan on Horseback,"
Ferdinand Victor Eugène Delacroix.
Drawing, *Figure 17–2.* Louvre, Paris.

given emphasis by using a double line for greater weight. Where small areas of light gray value or a texture have been desired, a simple back and forth scribble has been used (as in the eyebrows and the back of the collar). Make a series of such line drawings using forms that are not too symmetrical or regular. Organic forms, vegetables, fruits, leaves, or flowers make logical subjects since if contours deviate slightly from the model it will not spoil the drawing. Portraits and figure studies are more difficult than still life though they compensate because of their increased interest. If you wish, you can sketch your subject in light pencil lines before proceeding with ink. In such a case do not try to follow the pencil lines so closely that all freedom of movement is curtailed, but using the pencil lines as a general guide, draw in ink directly from the model. In using pen and ink care must be taken not to overload the pen. When this occurs, wipe the pen point against the side of the bottle before commencing to draw or the pen may deposit a large drop of ink when it first touches the paper. If you should have an accident with a drawing you like that has been done on good quality Bristol or illustration board, it is best to allow the ink to dry, scrape the excess ink off with a razor blade, and then with an ink eraser remove any remaining vestiges of the spot.

91. *Pen and ink cross-hatching. Detail of "Compositional Study," Pietro Testa. Drawing, Figures 4–3, 17–5.* Achenbach Foundation for Graphic Arts, California Palace of the Legion of Honor, San Francisco.

Project Sixty-eight

PEN AND INK: LINE DRAWINGS

The "Sultan on Horseback" by Delacroix (Figure 90) reveals considerably more technical sophistication than Figure 89. The Delacroix drawing was done rapidly, with a flourish that is reflected in the general exuberance of the drawing and in decided variations of thick and thin in the individual lines. In making drawings of this type one must be careful to avoid angular tails on the lines as one puts down or lifts the pen. This is accomplished by commencing the line movement while the hand is still in the air and lifting the hand while it is still in movement. Practice making sweeping movements, pen in hand, gradually bringing down and lifting the pen so that a line that is beautifully tapered at both ends is produced. Sketch a subject that does not demand exact contours; a figure or animal in action, a wrinkled drapery or garment thrown over a chair, a scribbled man, the trajectory of a movement, deep grass might be good subjects. Preliminary guide lines in hard pencil can be used if they are reassuring, but they should not be permitted to be restrictive or inhibiting.

92. Freely executed pen and ink cross-hatching.
Detail of "The Flight into Egypt,"
Gaspare Diziani. Drawing, Figure 4–9.
Museo Correr, Venice.

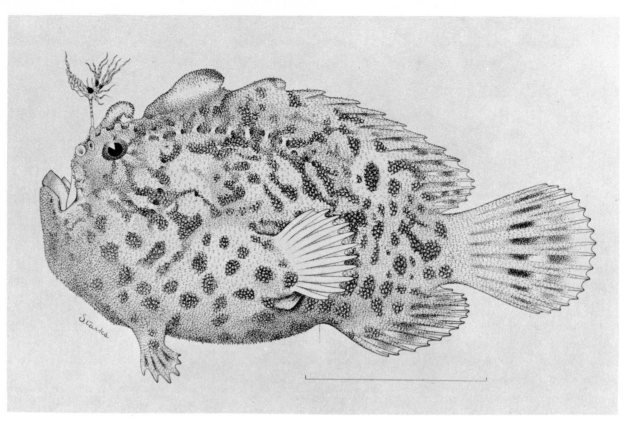

93a. *Pen and ink stippling
and formalized textures.
"Antennarius Tagus," Starks.
5¼" x 9¼".*
Collection of Dorothy Rich.

93b. *Detail of
"Antennarius Tagus."*

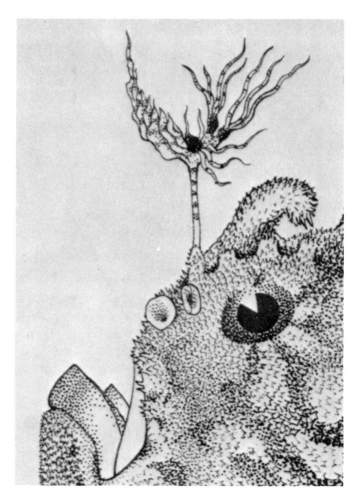

Project Sixty-nine

PEN AND INK: CROSS-HATCHING

The most usual way of building darker values in pen and ink is by cross-hatching. Cross-hatching is done by using a series of parallel lines at an angle to one another (Figure 91). Cross-hatching can be done with carefully applied lines which are evenly spaced or with almost scribbled sets of lines (Figure 92). It is important to have a fine quality smooth paper for cross-hatching or the surface of the paper will tear from repeated applications of the pen, become too absorbent, and the ink lines will blur.

Practice cross-hatching until you have some measure of control, then sketch a simple subject and proceed to model it in dark and light. At the beginning use simple forms which have clearly defined areas of dark and light and a minimum of surface texture. Simply formed light-colored fruit or vegetables, brilliantly lighted, are ideal for beginning exercises.

Project Seventy

PEN AND INK: STIPPLING AND PATTERN TEXTURES

Where very smooth gradations of value are desired, either to show form, texture or color pattern, as in scientific drawings, stippling and various formalized pattern textures are frequently used. In "Antennarius Tagus" (Figure 93a, b), combinations of lines and dots have been used with great skill and ingenuity to describe form and texture. You might find it interesting to repeat the exercise suggested as an introduction to texture (Project Forty-eight) in pen and ink, working to describe both form and texture in as disciplined a way as possible. A laboratory specimen from your biology or natural science class will also provide excellent subjects for this technique. When the areas of dark are not too extended, this technique proves most successful.

Pen and Ink: Texture Patterns
for Decorative Purposes

The use of pen and ink is also well adapted to drawings in which clearly defined patterns are desired, more for their expressive and decorative values than to describe form or surface texture. The "Head," by Ivan Majdrakoff (Figure 94), is built up largely from freely drawn triangular and circular linear patterns that have been extended, compressed, bent and twisted to create a great variety of movement and pattern effects. Using some simple kind of linear pattern as the basis of your texture, create a decorative composition. If you are at a loss for a subject, design a simple mask or head.

Project Seventy-one

PEN AND INK: PATTERN TEXTURES

In "The Survivor," by George Grosz (Figure 95), a rich variety of texture patterns has been used, both to describe form and surface character and for expressive effects. The pen and ink patterns reveal many varied uses of the pen, and some textures appear to have been produced by pressing fabrics or other materials which have been wet with ink against the paper. Experiment and see how many different texture patterns you can invent. Do not restrict your efforts to pen and brush, but try applying various textured materials dampened with ink to paper. When you have evolved an interesting group of texture patterns, carry out a composition using them. This technique is effective in a wide variety of situations and might be employed in an abstraction, an imaginative composition or a representational drawing.

Project Seventy-two

BRUSH AND INK

Pen and ink amplified by brush provides a transition between pure pen and ink and brush and ink drawing. Brush and ink is logical where more extended areas of dark are desired or lines with greater

94. *Pen and ink in formalized patterns.*
"Head," Majdrakoff. 9" x 10".
Collection of the author.

variation of width than can be achieved with the pen. "Madame Pierret," by Delacroix (Figure 96), provides an excellent example of brushed ink masses to supplement a pen drawing. Delacroix has maintained a consistent texture between the two media by using a simple linear transition to relate the blacks and whites. He has also reintroduced textured lights into such dark areas as hair. Because of the areas of dark, the drawing has great force and carries well. Select a subject with bold contrasts of dark and light and develop it with pen outlines, brushed ink darks, and use both pen and brush to create the transitional values and textures. A self-portrait done with strong light coming from one side might provide an effective subject.

■ Brush and Ink

The brush, when used with ink, provides both linear strength, bold masses of dark and light, and when used without a full load of ink, interesting dry-brush textures. You have already had introductory experiences in these uses of the brush so little need be said here except to point out that various kinds of brushes produce widely divergent effects. A stiff bristle brush, for instance, produces lines of a brusque, angular character, often with heavily dry-brushed edges. Chisel-shaped lettering brushes produce lines with sharp differences in width, depending upon whether the narrow or wide edge of the brush touches the paper, and so on. The long, very pointed Japanese brush is most responsive to pressures of the hand and so creates lines of unusually varied widths. Different papers also have much to do with the quality of line in brush drawing; soft absorbent papers like rice paper or blotting paper absorb the ink the moment the brush touches the paper and so create lines with much variation in width and in the character of edges. Hard-surfaced papers, on the other hand, absorb a minimum of ink from the brush, and this contributes to continuity of line and clean-cut edges. A dry-brush effect inevitably occurs in limited areas when a very roughly textured paper is used, and, conversely, it is almost impossible to achieve an interesting dry-brush quality with very smooth paper. Lastly, it should be noted that inks vary in opacity, viscosity and color, and that many artists

95. *Pen and ink texture-patterns.*
Detail of "The Survivor," George Grosz. Drawing, *Figure 15–15.*
Art Institute of Chicago (Gift of the Print and Drawing Club).

prefer tempera, oil paint, or printer's ink to India ink because they like being able to use their medium thick, for textured and dry-brush areas, and thinner when they desire a fluid medium that is responsive to the touch.

96. *Pen, brush and ink.*
"Madame Pierret," Ferdinand Victor
Eugène Delacroix (1798–1863;
French). Louvre, Paris

Project Seventy-three

BRUSH AND INK

Collect a variety of brushes, papers and media (partial sheets of paper and samples of media will suffice) and experiment with as many combinations as possible, exploring both line, mass and dry-brush textures. Make drawings using the combinations of brush and paper you find most interesting and satisfactory. Most brush and ink drawings are executed with rapidity, for the method of using brush and ink is not adapted to precision or careful elaboration of detail. For suggestions as to brush and ink technique, see Figures 9, 30, 31, 32.

97. *Japanese brush drawing.*
Detail of "The Old Woodcutter,"
Hokusai. Drawing, *Figure 13–4.*
Stanford Museum (Ikeda Collection).

Project Seventy-four

BRUSH AND INK: ORIENTAL CALLIGRAPHY

Among the most sophisticated and beautiful brush and ink drawings
are those by the Oriental masters. Long years of training in the manipulation of the brushes and learning the exact kinds of strokes
used in various situations constituted the traditional apprenticeship
for artists in the Orient. This careful apprenticeship provided the
basis for a virtuosity of performance that at best produced magnifi-
cent drawings but frequently was stultifying. Most Oriental brush
masters use a stick type of carbon ink (sumi) that is ground with
water on a shallow stone or ceramic type of block. This permits the
artist to control the density of the blacks. The brush is held in a
vertical position with the hand not touching the paper, which lays
flat. A very absorbent rice paper or silk ground is traditional, and by
raising and lowering the hand and loading the brush in varying degrees and in different ways (such as using the side, the tip alone,
heavy black ink in the tip, very thin, watery ink in the body of the
brush) effects of great diversity were produced. A good quality watercolor brush, blotter or rice paper, regular India ink, a saucer, and
water provide a substitute for the traditional materials for those
students wishing to explore this technique without purchasing the
special equipment. For an initial exploration you might attempt to
copy, on an enlarged scale, some parts of Figure 97 or details from
the Oriental brush drawing in *Drawing*, Figures 9–1, 2, 3, 7, 8, 9 or
11.

98. *Flat washes applied in clearly defined areas. Detail of "An Island in the Lagoon," Canaletto.* Drawing, *Figure 4–16.* Ashmolean Museum, Oxford. (*See also Plate 7.*)

■ *Wash Drawing*

A wash drawing is a painted drawing and as such it stands as a half-way step between drawing and painting. In wash drawing, intermediate values between black and white are achieved by diluting the ink or paint. Since the brush and the diluted medium are both extremely flexible vehicles, wash drawing provides for an unusual play of lines, values and textures (Figures 98, 99, 100, 101, 102). Wash has been the medium most used for study drawings in the periods when painterly effects were most highly valued. Many students have found wash provides a useful transition from drawing to painting.

The equipment is relatively simple; brush, ink, black watercolor or tempera, and water. (If oil paint or printer's ink is used, turpentine or thinner provides the dilutant. For the remainder of this discussion it will be assumed that a water-solvent medium is being used.) Wash drawing should be done on an absorbent paper that is not too thin, as thin papers wrinkle and buckle when they are wet. Regular watercolor paper of a good quality or illustration board are most satisfactory. Illustration board can be thumbtacked to your drawing board, watercolor paper is best mounted. To mount watercolor paper, wet it thoroughly on both sides, lay it on the board for about five minutes until the water has been absorbed, smooth out slightly, and fasten the edges of the paper down with butcher tape (not masking tape). Allow to dry, at which time buckling will disappear. This holds the watercolor paper flat, keeps it from swelling and therefore minimizes the pooling of your washes.

In addition to the equipment and materials indicated above, you will need a quantity of clean water close by your work table and a supply of absorbent paint rags. A sponge is also useful for wetting the paper or for picking up areas of wash that appear too dark. A white saucer, plate or watercolor palette provides a surface for mixing your pigment.

Project Seventy-five

WASH DRAWING: FLAT WASHES

If you are using a number 8 or 10 watercolor brush, as has been previously suggested, keep your first wash drawing about the size of this study guide. While wash is best adapted to a free and spontaneous handling, a rather cautious and systematic procedure may be advisable for students who have never previously worked in watercolor or wash, in which case select a subject with clearly defined planes of dark and light. An architectural subject may work well. Draw in your subject with firm outlines, either in pencil or pen and ink. Plan the distribution of your values. Leave pure white paper for your lightest areas. Put a couple of tablespoons of water in your saucer (or palette) and add enough ink or paint to make a light gray. Fill your brush with this gray and spread it over all the areas which you plan to be other than white. When this wash is dry, add a second wash of gray to the next darkest area. Continue until you have worked down to your darkest area. As you work toward the darks you may wish to make your puddle of gray darker than at the start as this enables you to achieve the strongest darks more rapidly. Never try to lay a wash over a partially dry surface as this produces an ugly mottled effect. A detail from "An Island in the Lagoon" (Figure 98) by Canaletto provides an example by a master of this relatively controlled type of wash drawing.

Project Seventy-six

WASH DRAWING: MODULATED AREAS

Wash is particularly well adapted to free and fluid effects. Wash drawings can be done directly on the paper without evidence of preliminary drawings (Figure 99) or can be combined with pencil (Figure 100), pen and ink (Figure 101), charcoal (Figure 102) or almost any nongreasy drawing medium. When combined with other media, it is the artist's option whether the wash precede or follow the pencil, pen, or charcoal lines. The degree to which the linear elements become incorporated into the wash drawing is also according to the preference of the artist. Select a subject which permits a somewhat splashy, spontaneous effect. A landscape, still life, life drawing or freely rendered illustration provides a good subject. Many magazine cartoons are done in wash drawing. In contrast to Project Seventy-five, try for free and spontaneous, painterly effects (Figure 101). Sketch your subject in the medium of your choice. Keep your concentrated ink or paint accessible, and mix a fair-sized puddle of middle-value gray in your palette. Proceed to paint, adding water to your middle-value gray when you want lighter tones, and concentrated paint when you want darker ones. Do not try to get flat washes or smooth effects, but permit the brush strokes and movements of paint from thinner washes to thicker to show. When once washes have commenced to dry, allow surfaces to become completely dry before you try to add additional layers of wash. Last add your most concentrated accents of black. If you want to recover some

99. *Wash applied directly without reinforcing lines.*
Detail of "The Tiber Above Rome," Claude Lorrain. Drawing, Figure 17–10.
Trustees of the British Museum, London. (*See also Plate 16.*)

small areas of white which have been covered with wash, you can retouch with opaque tempera white. If you want clearly defined edges in a wash, apply it to a dry surface; if you want softened contours (as in drawing clouds), wet the paper first with your sponge and lay the wash into the wet surface.

Project Seventy-seven

WASH DRAWING

Wash may be combined with pure pen lines, with brush lines or in combination with cross-hatch, stippled, dry-brush textures, and most other previously discussed techniques. Frequently, wash provides a convenient way to unify a composition that appears to lack cohesiveness. If you have found a way of using pen and ink or brush and ink that is particularly to your liking, start a composition using that technique, planning to combine it with wash. Let us assume you settle on cross-hatched pen and ink and wash as in Figure 101. Develop your composition partially in pen line, then add wash. Return to pen and ink and add cross-hatched pen lines where they will strengthen the form. If it will contribute to the richness of the drawing, add more wash, more cross-hatching, and so on. If you lose your lights, they can be reintroduced either by scratching out lights with a razor blade or by using white tempera paint.

■ Mixed Media

In *Drawing* we read: "Some artists are purists by temperament and take the limitations of a medium as a challenge. Such men delight in bending the medium to their esthetic will and making it do what seems impossible. . . . Other artists care only to achieve a certain effect, and they freely combine media to realize their goals. Many drawings by both old and modern masters were not commenced with clearly defined plans as to media but instead were improvised as they developed. Such drawings were frequently started in a medium which was well adapted to an initial exploration, such as charcoal or chalk. At a certain step an artist may add wash. Ink may then be used to intensify the darks and subsequently white tempera added to strengthen the lights; a small amount of colored chalk may provide a final enrichment." Study your previous works. If you find a drawing from your earlier studies which did not realize its full potential and which you feel might be improved or enriched by working on it in another medium, proceed to do so. Colored chalks, ink, wash, and tempera can be added to charcoal—ink, wash, colored chalks, to pencil, and so forth. You might also profit from starting a drawing in pencil on illustration board with no preconceptions as to how you will complete it, and then proceed to develop it with whatever media and materials seem appropriate as you go along.

100. *Wash reinforced with pencil.*
Detail of "Rock Quarry," Caspar David Friedrich.
Drawing, *Figure 16–6.* National Gallery, Berlin.

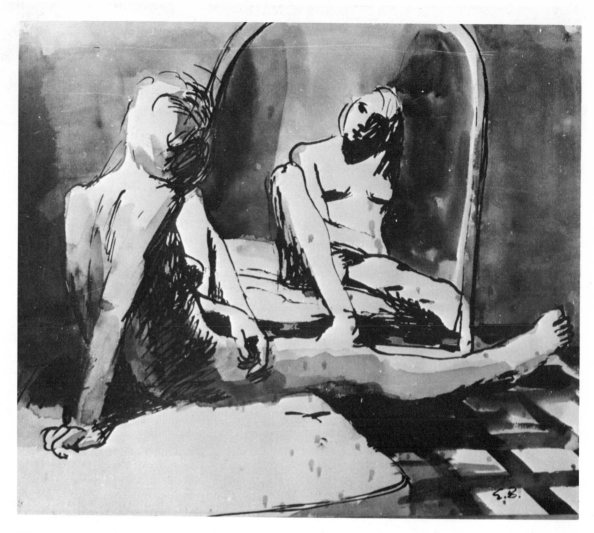

101. *Pen and ink with wash.
"Seated Figure Reflected in
a Mirror," Elmer Bischoff.
San Francisco Museum of Art.*

Project Seventy-eight

NEW MATERIALS AND MEDIA: EXPLORATION

On page 416 of *Drawing* there is an extensive list of media compiled
from a single recent exhibition of drawings. On page 417 there is an
equally interesting list taken from a catalogue of works by Paul Klee.
Each year the manufacturers of art materials and stationery supplies
introduce new equipment and materials that are adaptable for drawing purposes. Certain recent developments have already become
standard art equipment; felt pens, ball-point pens, nylon-tipped pens,
for instance, provide for a wide range of line widths in many colors.
Recent rubber emulsions developed as friskets to protect areas of
white paper from washes, ink, other water-solvent paints and soiling
are now used for their brilliant "stopped out" effects. To be inventive
in the uses and combinations of materials is of great importance for
it encourages the artist to avoid artistic clichés. Waxed crayon or
rubber cement used under wash produces effects similar to the fris-

102. *Charcoal and wash.*
Detail of "Drawing for Sacrifice," Jacques Lipschitz.
Drawing, *Figure 10–3.* San Francisco Museum of Art.

103. *Ink applied to paper with corduroy. 5″ x 6″.*

kets mentioned above, but the rubber cement results in a very different and unique line quality, while white crayon creates interesting granular surfaces. Even the most traditional materials, in the hands of an inventive person, take on fresh and original uses. For instance, drawings done in chalk, charcoal, or pencil tones, in which the lights are achieved by erasing rather than by leaving white paper, have their own unique textural effects (Figure 102). Ink applied to paper with a piece of corduroy creates a curious variation of cross-hatching (Figure 103). Even drawing with the left hand, assuming you are right-handed, develops new linear and textural qualities, since the habits of hand movement that become "built in" to the drawing act are disrupted. The result is less skilled, but consequently fresh linear and pattern qualities often ensue.

A few simple experiences may encourage the habit of exploration. Select the experiments that appeal to you from the following: (1) Draw some simple object in a familiar medium with the hand you do not ordinarily use for drawing. (2) Roll a small piece of heavily textured cloth into a compact ball. Wet it slightly with ink and press it against a piece of paper. Make a dark and light drawing using only the fabric ball dampened with ink to build your value patterns. If you want sharp edges, cut out a stencil. (3) Rub a middle value coat of powdered charcoal into a piece of paper. Do a drawing in erased lights, adding darks and erasing lights until your drawing is completed. (4) Make a drawing on firm white paper with rubber cement. It is viscous and stringy, so do not attempt to achieve smoothly modulated lines, but accept its unpredictable irregularities. Lay a wash of mottled gray over the entire drawing, and when the wash is dry, rub off the rubber cement. If the resulting white pattern pleases you, consider the drawing completed. If you feel it necessary, add darks which will complement the white pattern. (5) Do a large drawing with a felt-tip pen or commercial laundry marking pen, using cross-hatch or some other technique for which you ordinarily employ a fine pen point. Dramatize the bold scale that results as effectively as possible. (6) More important than any of the above suggestions, doodle and play on paper with some medium you find intriguing. Make a drawing from something that occurs in the course of your playful explorations.

part 4

IMAGINATION

C HAPTER 18, Imagination, in *Drawing* we read "Imagination is multifaceted and there is no aspect of creation, even on the pure craft level, where the play of imagination is not necessary to achieve the heightened powers of communication that characterizes the arts." Imaginative invention is present in every person to some degree in the form of daydreaming. Translating imaginative potential into patterns of creativity is developed and reinforced by habits of doing. The following exercises are suggested in the hope that you may discover potentialities in yourself hitherto neglected.

Project Seventy-nine

IMAGINATION: ASPECTS OF THE IMAGINATIVE ACT

In the chapter on Imagination in *Drawing*, four aspects of the imaginative act are identified: the ability (1) to empathize, (2) to fantasize, (3) to particularize, (4) to generalize. These aspects of imagination are not mutually exclusive of one another, but for the sake of conceptual awareness they are here assigned as four separate activities. (1) To empathize. Take some object for which you have a strong feeling of sympathy (a faded flower, a dejected tramp, a playful kitten, a sentimental valentine, a worn toy). Draw it with what you feel to be the proper sympathetic mood: a careless abandon, a harsh tense stroke, compulsive care and precision. Next try using conscious exaggerations of line movement, of dark and light or texture which will communicate your feelings more forcefully than would an objective drawing. (2) To fantasize. Create a fantastic creature by combining attributes from the following: human, bird and fish, insect, automobile and airplane. Other possibilities are (1) draw a dream, or (2) use free-association: start with no preconceptions and improvise as you go along. If your mind rejects these suggestions in favor of others, you are moving in the right direction. Follow your own impulse. (3) To particularize. Draw a caricature of your face. Try to exaggerate the characterizing features so the drawing is unmistakably you. If you prefer, do a caricature of a friend from memory. (4) To generalize: Create an impersonal symbol of animal, bird, insect, or machine. Avoid having your symbol look like any particular animal or bird, insect or machine, but rather try to evolve a form that conveys the attributes of the category. Another suggestion is to draw a series of masks which symbolize (1) beauty, (2) nobility, (3) brutality, or (4) evil.

Project Eighty

IMAGINATION: SELECTIVITY AND EMPHASIS

Figures 104a, b, c and d show four possible arrangements which might be employed by an artist drawing a tree upon a hilltop. If the hilltop is placed high on the page with the tree small against the sky, one immediately senses the long slope of hill, the profile of a hilltop interrupted by the accent of the tree (Figure 104a). The same hilltop and same-sized tree placed low on the page conveys a sense of the vastness of the sky, big because of the small tree, the unbroken

expanse of sky emphasized by the sinuous line of the hill and the
undulating and broken surface of the earth (Figure 104b).

Perhaps the massive strength of the tree is what impresses the artist,
in which case he might draw it close up, and placing it in the middle
of the page, stress the weighty trunk and the powerful branches by
allowing the central mass of the tree to fill the entire page (Figure
104c). Or the artist may be most concerned with the way the pre-
vailing winds have shaped and broken the branches, and so he selects

104b. *Tree on a hilltop. "Oak," D. Mendelowitz. Nylon point and ball-point pen, 6" x 7½".* Collection of the author.

104c. *Tree and sky. "Oak," D. Mendelowitz. Nylon point and ball-point pen, 6" x 7½".* Collection of the author.

104d. *Composition with detail of oak.*
"Oak," D. Mendelowitz. Nylon point
and ball-point pen, 6" x 7½". Collection of the author.

a section of the tree in which strong diagonal and horizontal lines dominate the composition and the absence of other than a few scattered masses of leaves suggests the wind-torn struggle for existence that has given the tree its particular character (Figure 104d). Here high, low, close up and still more close up means selection and emphasis, and thereby provides the basis for stressing the particular aspects of the tree which attracted the artist. Imaginative play with various compositional arrangements made it possible to arrive at Figure 104c, the drawing of this particular tree that was most satisfying to the artist and therefore expressive of the artist's insight. Go through your drawings and select one that does not seem to do justice to the subject. Or select a fresh subject. In a series of small rectangles (2 inches by 3 inches) plan thumbnail sketches of various arrangements. Select the one which seems most successful in communicating your feeling about the subject and make a full-scale drawing of it. Compare it with the original. The habit of making thumbnail sketches before starting a drawing provides for the rapid visualization of a projected composition and encourages the imaginative exploration of a subject before the arrangement is "fixed." A similar use of the thumbnail sketch enables an artist to develop an idea through a sequence of steps (Figure 105).

Project Eighty-one

IMAGINATIVE IMPROVISATION

Imaginative play in artistic expression often takes the form of elaborating a simple and familiar motif. In "Ten Numbers" (Figure 106), Jaspar Johns has enriched the simple arabic numbers by a playful texturing of background areas. Almost any familiar shape or object can provide the subject for visual improvisation, in the same way that a simple melodic theme can initiate elaborate musical invention. Select an object, a pattern, or a symbol from a source you do not ordinarily think of as an artistic resource (the supermarket, the newspaper, a service station, and so on) and see in how many ways you can utilize the motif in a sequence of textural or pattern inventions.

Project Eighty-two

IMAGINATION: THE ART ELEMENTS

In *Drawing,* page 437, it is conjectured that the inspiration for a drawing by Paul Klee titled "Costumed Puppets" (Figure 18–17) was the flattened line ending in a spiral from which the drawing was constructed. Doodle until you create a motif that appeals to you, or choose a line, texture, form or pattern from an existent work of art or some other source. Cracks on plaster walls, the patterns on stained walls, a string dipped in ink and dropped on a piece of paper, ink blots, rubbings, and so on, can also provide starting points for an esthetic creation. Using the medium of your choice draw your motif on a piece of paper and proceed to improvise. If you feel like making an identifiable object, do so. If you wish to develop an elaborate doodle, follow that impulse. Let the dynamics of your imagination determine what you do with your initial stimulus. If nothing happens, it does not follow that you are unimaginative but merely that this procedure does not provide the proper stimulus for you.

Project Eighty-three

IMAGINATION: MATERIALS

Imagination is reflected as much in how one draws as in what. The imaginative person thinks of unconventional uses for materials, of unorthodox combinations of media and extends the boundaries of technique through his inventive behavior. In Project Seventy-eight, New Materials and Media, Exploration (p. 140), some new materials and ways of handling more conventional drawing materials are suggested. If that assignment stimulated new directions you would like to explore, take this opportunity to do so. Or visit an art supply store and see if you can discover unfamiliar media or materials that intrigue you. Experiment with them and see if you can expand your technical resources.

105. *Sequential development*
of a pictorial idea
through thumbnail sketches.
Detail of "The Cow,"
Theo van Doesburg.
Drawing, Figure 18–2.
Museum of Modern Art, New York.

106. *Improvisation on a familiar theme.*
Detail of "Numbers," Jasper Johns.
Drawing, *Figure 12–11.*
Collection of Mr. Ted Carey.

Imagination and Artistic Stimuli

The imaginative functions of no two individuals are identical, for imagination stems from the deepest layers of pesronality. Certain personalities are stimulated to a high level of imaginative activity by the external living world about them; others find their chief stimulus in the world of art: A piece of music, reading a book, seeing a play or viewing paintings or drawings brings on a heightened mood of elation which is most effectively discharged by creative activity. If you feel that you are stimulated by works of art, expose yourself to a stimulating artistic experience before you start your next drawing. Then undertake your drawing project while you are still in a heightened emotional mood. The project may or may not be related in subject or manner to the artistic catalyzer.